Mastering Three.js: A Journey Through 3D Web Development

Kameron Hussain and Frahaan Hussain

Published by Sonar Publishing, 2023.

MASTERING THREE.JS: A JOURNEY THROUGH 3D WEB DEVELOPMENT

First edition. December 9, 2023.

ISBN: 979-8223854814

Written by Kameron Hussain and Frahaan Hussain.

Table of Contents

Backup and Redundancy

Scalability

Cost Management

20.5 Post-Launch Maintenance and Updates

Bug Fixes

Security Updates

Browser Compatibility

Performance Optimization

Content Updates

Compatibility with New Three.js Versions

Backup and Disaster Recovery

User Support and Documentation

Analytics and User Feedback

Version Control and Testing

Compliance and Regulations

User Engagement and Marketing

Chapter 1: Introduction to Three.js

1.1. Understanding Three.js and Its Place in Web Development

Three.js is a powerful and versatile JavaScript library that enables developers to create and display animated 3D graphics in a web browser, without the need for plugins. This library is built upon WebGL (Web Graphics Library), a JavaScript API that renders high-performance 3D and 2D graphics within any compatible web browser without the use of plug-ins.

The inception of Three.js marked a significant milestone in web development. It opened doors for developers and designers to experiment with 3D graphics, bringing a new dimension to user interfaces, data visualization, and interactive web experiences. The importance of Three.js in modern web development stems from its ability to harness the capabilities of WebGL in a more accessible and easier-to-understand format.

Key Features of Three.js

- **Simplicity**: Three.js abstracts many of the complexities of WebGL, making it more approachable for those new to 3D programming.

- **Extensibility**: The library provides numerous extensions and plugins, allowing for the creation of complex 3D environments and effects.

- **Community Support**: With a large and active community, developers have access to a wealth of resources, examples, and support.

Getting Started with Three.js

To begin with Three.js, you need to set up a basic development environment. This typically involves:

1. **HTML Structure**: A simple HTML file to host your 3D content.
2. **JavaScript Setup**: Linking the Three.js library in your project, either by downloading the library or linking to a CDN.

```
<!DOCTYPE html>

<html>

<head>

<title>My First Three.js App</title>

<style>

body { margin: 0; }

canvas { width: 100%; height: 100% }

</style>

</head>

<body>

<script src="https://cdnjs.cloudflare.com/ajax/libs/three.js/r128/three.min.js"></script>

<script>

// Three.js code goes here
```

```
</script>

</body>

</html>
```

Core Components of a Three.js Scene

In Three.js, a scene is composed of several core components:

- **Scene**: The container for all your objects, cameras, and lights.
- **Camera**: Provides a perspective through which we see the scene.
- **Renderer**: Renders the scene using WebGL and displays it on a canvas element in the webpage.

Creating a Basic Scene

To create a basic Three.js scene, the following steps are followed:

1. **Initialize the Scene**: Create a new Three.js scene object.
2. **Set Up the Camera**: Define the perspective.
3. **Create a Renderer**: Assign a renderer to draw the scene.

```
const scene = new THREE.Scene();

const camera = new THREE.PerspectiveCamera(75, window.innerWidth/window.innerHeight, 0.1, 1000);

const renderer = new THREE.WebGLRenderer();

renderer.setSize(window.innerWidth, window.innerHeight);

document.body.appendChild(renderer.domElement);
```

Adding a 3D Object

The most basic form of 3D object in Three.js is a mesh, which is created using geometry (shape) and material (appearance). For instance, to create a simple cube:

```
const geometry = new THREE.BoxGeometry();

const material = new THREE.MeshBasicMaterial({ color: 0x00ff00 });

const cube = new THREE.Mesh(geometry, material);

scene.add(cube);

camera.position.z = 5;
```

Animation Loop

To animate the scene, you need to create a render loop. This loop continuously renders the scene, allowing for animations and interactions.

```
function animate() {

requestAnimationFrame(animate);

// Update the scene

cube.rotation.x += 0.01;

cube.rotation.y += 0.01;

// Render the scene

renderer.render(scene, camera);

}
```

animate();

Conclusion

This section provided an introductory overview of Three.js, covering its significance in web development, basic setup, and the creation of a simple 3D scene. As you progress through this book, you'll delve deeper into these concepts, exploring more complex geometries, materials, animations, and interactions that are possible with Three.js. The next section will explore the evolution of 3D graphics in web browsers, giving you a deeper understanding of how technologies like WebGL and Three.js have transformed the web experience.

1.2. The Evolution of 3D Graphics in Web Browsers

The evolution of 3D graphics in web browsers is a story of technological innovation and the relentless pursuit of more immersive and interactive web experiences. This journey, spanning several decades, has seen significant advancements in both hardware and software technologies, leading to the sophisticated web graphics we see today.

Early Days: The Beginnings of Web Graphics

In the early days of the internet, web graphics were predominantly two-dimensional, ranging from simple images and animations to basic interactivities created with technologies like Adobe Flash and Java applets. These technologies provided a platform for richer visual content but were limited in their capabilities, especially in rendering 3D graphics.

The Advent of WebGL

The real game-changer in web graphics was the introduction of WebGL. WebGL, short for Web Graphics Library, is a JavaScript API that allows for rendering interactive 3D graphics within any compatible web browser, without the need for plugins. It was developed as a web standard by the Khronos Group, an industry consortium.

Key Advantages of WebGL

- **Plugin-Free**: Runs natively in the browser, eliminating the need for external plugins.
- **Hardware Acceleration**: Utilizes the power of the user's graphics processing unit (GPU), allowing for more complex and high-quality graphics.
- **Accessibility**: Made 3D graphics more accessible to web developers, not just specialized graphics programmers.

Impact of WebGL on Web Development

The advent of WebGL marked a significant shift in what was possible in terms of web graphics. Developers could now create sophisticated 3D environments, leading to applications in gaming, data visualization, and even virtual and augmented reality experiences.

Rise of Three.js and Other Libraries

To make WebGL more accessible, libraries like Three.js were developed. These libraries abstracted much of the complexity of WebGL, providing a simpler, higher-level API for developers to work with. This made 3D web development more approachable and opened the doors for creative exploration.

Evolution of Browser Performance

As web graphics became more advanced, browsers also evolved to support these changes. Browser vendors continuously improved their graphics engines to handle WebGL content more efficiently. This led to better performance, higher frame rates, and smoother animations, even on less powerful devices.

Integration with HTML and CSS

3D graphics in web browsers are not standalone; they need to integrate seamlessly with other web technologies like HTML and CSS. This integration allows for the creation of holistic web experiences where 3D content complements the traditional web elements.

Examples of Advanced 3D Web Applications

- **Interactive 3D Websites**: Websites with immersive 3D environments that users can navigate and interact with.

- **Web-Based Games**: Leveraging WebGL and Three.js to create graphically rich online games.

- **Data Visualization**: Using 3D graphics to represent complex data in an interactive and intuitive manner.

- **Virtual Reality (VR) and Augmented Reality (AR)**: Creating immersive VR and AR experiences directly in the browser.

Challenges and Limitations

Despite its advancements, 3D graphics in web browsers face challenges:

- **Performance**: High-quality 3D graphics can be resource-intensive, requiring optimization to run smoothly on all devices.

- **Cross-Browser Compatibility**: Ensuring consistent performance across different web browsers.

- **Learning Curve**: While libraries like Three.js have made it easier, 3D web development still has a steeper learning curve compared to traditional web development.

Future of 3D Graphics in Web Browsers

The future of 3D graphics in web browsers is promising. With continuous advancements in web standards, improvements in browser performance, and the increasing power of graphics hardware, the possibilities for 3D graphics on the web are expanding. We can expect more immersive, interactive, and visually stunning web experiences in the years to come.

Conclusion

This section outlined the evolution of 3D graphics in web browsers, highlighting key milestones and technologies like WebGL and Three.js. The journey from simple 2D graphics to sophisticated 3D environments reflects the dynamic nature of web development and points to an exciting future for web-based 3D graphics. As you move forward in this book, you'll gain a deeper understanding of these technologies and how you can leverage them to create engaging and interactive 3D web experiences.

1.3. Setting Up the Development Environment

Setting up a proper development environment is crucial for efficient and effective Three.js development. This section will guide you through the process of creating an environment tailored for developing 3D web applications using Three.js.

Choosing a Code Editor

The first step is to choose a code editor. There are several popular options available:

- **Visual Studio Code (VS Code)**: A widely used editor with excellent support for JavaScript and numerous extensions.

- **Sublime Text**: Known for its speed and efficiency, it's another great choice for web development.

- **Atom**: An open-source editor that's highly customizable.

Installing Node.js and npm

Node.js is a runtime environment that lets you run JavaScript on the server side. npm, which stands for Node Package Manager, is used to manage dependencies in your project. To install Node.js and npm:

1. Visit the Node.js website[1].

1. https://nodejs.org/

2. Download and install the version recommended for most users.
3. Verify the installation by running node -v and npm -v in your terminal or command prompt.

Setting Up a Three.js Project

To set up a basic Three.js project, follow these steps:

1. **Create a New Project Directory**: Make a new folder for your project and navigate into it.
2. **Initialize npm**: Run npm init in your terminal and follow the prompts to create a package.json file.
3. **Install Three.js**: Execute npm install three to add Three.js to your project.

Basic Project Structure

Your project should have a basic structure:

- index.html: Your main HTML file.
- src/: A directory for your JavaScript source files.
- styles/: A directory for your CSS files.

Sample index.html File

Here's a basic index.html template:

```
<!DOCTYPE html>

<html lang="en">

<head>

<meta charset="UTF-8">
```

```
<meta name="viewport" content="width=device-width, initial-scale=1.0">

<title>Three.js Project</title>

<link rel="stylesheet" href="styles/main.css">

</head>

<body>

<script src="src/app.js"></script>

</body>

</html>
```

Creating a main.css File

In the styles folder, create a main.css file:

```
body {

margin: 0;

overflow: hidden;

}
```

Writing Your First Three.js Script

In the src folder, create an app.js file. This file will contain your Three.js code. For example:

```
import * as THREE from 'three';

const scene = new THREE.Scene();

// Add your Three.js code here
```

Using a Local Development Server

For development, it's beneficial to use a local server:

- **http-server**: A simple, zero-configuration command-line http server.
- **live-server**: Provides live reload capability.

To install http-server, run npm install -g http-server and start it in your project directory using http-server.

Version Control with Git

Using Git for version control is highly recommended. Initialize Git in your project directory by running git init and make regular commits to track and manage changes.

Debugging Tools

- **Browser Developer Tools**: Use the console, debugger, and network tabs for debugging.
- **Three.js DevTools**: An extension for Chrome that provides insights into Three.js scenes.

Additional Tools and Libraries

As you progress, you might want to incorporate additional tools and libraries like:

- **Webpack**: A module bundler.
- **Babel**: A JavaScript compiler for using next-generation JavaScript, today.

- **Three.js Inspector**: An extension for debugging Three.js scenes.

Conclusion

Setting up a well-structured development environment is key to a smooth and productive coding experience. This setup, encompassing a code editor, Node.js, npm, and a local server, provides a strong foundation for developing Three.js applications. With your environment ready, you're set to start building immersive 3D web experiences. The next sections will delve deeper into the core components of Three.js and how to use them effectively.

1.4. Core Components of Three.js

Understanding the core components of Three.js is fundamental to building any 3D web application. This section will explore these components, explaining their roles and how they interact to create a 3D scene.

The Scene

The scene in Three.js is the starting point of any 3D world. It acts as a container in which all objects, lights, and cameras are placed. Think of it as an empty stage where you add your 3D models, lights, and cameras.

```
const scene = new THREE.Scene();
```

Cameras

The camera in Three.js defines what is visible in the scene. There are several types of cameras in Three.js, but the most commonly used one is the PerspectiveCamera, which simulates human vision.

```
const camera = new THREE.PerspectiveCamera(75, window.innerWidth / window.innerHeight, 0.1, 1000);

camera.position.set(0, 0, 5);

scene.add(camera);
```

Renderers

The renderer takes the scene and a camera and displays them to the canvas of a web page. The WebGLRenderer is the most widely used renderer in Three.js.

```
const renderer = new THREE.WebGLRenderer();

renderer.setSize(window.innerWidth, window.innerHeight);

document.body.appendChild(renderer.domElement);
```

Meshes

Meshes are objects that you can add to your scene. They are made up of two parts: geometry (shape) and material (appearance).

```
const geometry = new THREE.BoxGeometry();

const material = new THREE.MeshBasicMaterial({ color: 0x00ff00 });

const cube = new THREE.Mesh(geometry, material);

scene.add(cube);
```

Geometries

Geometries define the shape of objects in Three.js. There are many predefined geometries like BoxGeometry, SphereGeometry, and CylinderGeometry.

Materials

Materials define the appearance of objects. Three.js provides several types of materials, such as MeshBasicMaterial, MeshLambertMaterial, and MeshPhongMaterial, each with its own characteristics and uses.

Lights

Lighting is crucial in a 3D scene to provide depth and realism. Three.js offers various types of lights, including ambient, point, directional, and spotlights.

```
const light = new THREE.PointLight(0xffffff, 1, 100);

light.position.set(10, 10, 10);

scene.add(light);
```

Animation

To create animations in Three.js, you can update properties of objects, camera, or materials in the render loop.

```
function animate() {

requestAnimationFrame(animate);

cube.rotation.x += 0.01;

cube.rotation.y += 0.01;
```

renderer.render(scene, camera);

}

animate();

Loaders

Loaders in Three.js are used to import external models and textures. For example, the GLTFLoader is commonly used to load 3D models in the glTF format.

Controls

For interactive scenes, Three.js provides control libraries like OrbitControls for rotating and zooming the camera around a specific point.

const controls = **new** THREE.OrbitControls(camera, renderer.domElement);

Event Listeners

Event listeners can be used to make the scene interactive. You can listen to mouse and keyboard events to trigger changes in the scene.

Raycasting

Raycasting is used for mouse picking, where you can detect which objects in the 3D scene are under the mouse pointer.

Helper Objects

Three.js comes with several helper objects like GridHelper, AxisHelper, and CameraHelper to aid in the development process.

Performance Optimization

It's important to manage memory and resources efficiently to ensure the performance of your 3D application, especially when dealing with complex scenes.

Best Practices

- **Modularity**: Keep your code modular for better maintainability.

- **Asset Management**: Efficiently manage and load assets to reduce load times.

- **Responsive Design**: Ensure your 3D application is responsive to different screen sizes.

Conclusion

These core components form the basis of any application built using Three.js. Understanding and effectively utilizing them is key to creating compelling and interactive 3D web experiences. As you advance through the book, you'll delve deeper into each of these components, exploring their capabilities and learning how to use them to their full potential.

1.5. First Steps: Creating a Basic Three.js Scene

Creating a basic Three.js scene is the first step toward mastering 3D web graphics. This section will guide you through the process of setting up a simple scene, which includes a cube, a camera, and some basic lighting.

Setting Up the HTML File

Start by creating an HTML file that will serve as the canvas for your Three.js scene:

```
<!DOCTYPE html>

<html>

<head>

<title>Basic Three.js Scene</title>

<style>

body { margin: 0; }

canvas { display: block; }

</style>

</head>

<body>

<script src="https://cdnjs.cloudflare.com/ajax/libs/three.js/r128/three.min.js"></script>

<script src="app.js"></script>

</body>

</html>
```

Writing the JavaScript: app.js

In your JavaScript file, you will set up the basic components of a Three.js scene: scene, camera, renderer, geometry, material, and mesh.

Initializing the Scene

Create a new Three.js scene:

```
const scene = new THREE.Scene();
```

Adding the Camera

Define a perspective camera:

```
const camera = new THREE.PerspectiveCamera(75, window.innerWidth / window.innerHeight, 0.1, 1000);

camera.position.z = 5;
```

Creating the Renderer

Set up the WebGL renderer:

```
const renderer = new THREE.WebGLRenderer();

renderer.setSize(window.innerWidth, window.innerHeight);

document.body.appendChild(renderer.domElement);
```

Handling Window Resize

Ensure the scene adjusts when the window is resized:

```
window.addEventListener('resize', () => {

renderer.setSize(window.innerWidth, window.innerHeight);

camera.aspect = window.innerWidth / window.innerHeight;

camera.updateProjectionMatrix();
```

```
});
```

Creating a Cube

Define geometry, material, and create a mesh:

```
const geometry = new THREE.BoxGeometry();

const material = new THREE.MeshBasicMaterial({ color: 0x00ff00 });

const cube = new THREE.Mesh(geometry, material);

scene.add(cube);
```

Adding Lighting

Although not mandatory for MeshBasicMaterial, let's add a simple ambient light:

```
const light = new THREE.AmbientLight(0xffffff); // soft white light

scene.add(light);
```

Creating the Animation Loop

Animate the cube with a simple rotation:

```
function animate() {

requestAnimationFrame(animate);

cube.rotation.x += 0.01;

cube.rotation.y += 0.01;
```

```
renderer.render(scene, camera);
}
animate();
```

Understanding the Components

In this setup:

- **Scene**: Acts as a container for all your objects, cameras, and lights.
- **Camera**: Defines the point of view from which the scene is rendered.
- **Renderer**: Renders the scene using the camera's perspective and displays it on a canvas.
- **Mesh**: Consists of geometry (the shape of the object) and material (how it looks).

Experimenting with the Scene

Try changing the cube's color or size, adjust the camera position, or experiment with different geometries like THREE.SphereGeometry.

Debugging and Testing

Use browser developer tools to debug your code. Console logs and breakpoints are helpful to understand how your scene is rendered.

Expanding Your Scene

As you get comfortable, start adding more objects, different types of lights, and experiment with different camera settings.

Performance Considerations

Keep an eye on the performance as you add more elements. Use tools like the Three.js inspector for Chrome to analyze and optimize your scene.

Learning Through Experimentation

The best way to learn Three.js is by experimenting with various components and observing how they affect the scene.

Conclusion

This section provided a step-by-step guide to creating a basic Three.js scene. Through this process, you learned about the essential components like scenes, cameras, renderers, geometries, materials, and lighting. As you progress through the book, you will build upon this foundation, exploring more complex 3D objects, animations, and interactivity in Three.js.

Chapter 2: The Fundamentals of 3D Graphics

2.1. Understanding 3D Coordinate Systems

A fundamental aspect of working with 3D graphics in Three.js, and in any 3D environment, is understanding the 3D coordinate system. This coordinate system is the framework upon which all 3D objects and scenes are built and manipulated.

The Basics of 3D Coordinates

In 3D graphics, coordinates are defined with three values, typically referred to as X, Y, and Z:

- **X-Axis**: Usually represents left and right.
- **Y-Axis**: Generally stands for up and down.
- **Z-Axis**: Often signifies depth, with positive values coming out of the screen towards the viewer.

Visualizing the Coordinate System

Imagine the 3D space as a room, where the origin (0, 0, 0) is at the center. Objects can be placed relative to this center point in all three dimensions.

Positioning Objects in Three.js

When creating objects in Three.js, you position them using these three coordinates. For example, placing a cube at (1, 2, 3):

```
cube.position.set(1, 2, 3);
```

The Right-Hand Rule

Three.js uses the right-hand coordinate system, which means if you hold up your right hand, your thumb points along the X-axis, your index finger along the Y-axis, and your middle finger along the Z-axis.

Understanding Vector3

Three.js uses the Vector3 class to represent a point in 3D space. This is not just for positions but also used in scales, rotations, and other 3D operations.

```
const point = new THREE.Vector3(1, 2, 3);
```

Transformations: Translation, Rotation, Scale

In 3D graphics, there are three primary types of transformations:

1. **Translation**: Moving an object in 3D space.
2. **Rotation**: Rotating an object around the three axes.
3. **Scale**: Changing the size of an object.

Translation in Three.js

Moving an object involves changing its position along the X, Y, and Z axes.

```
object.position.x += 1; // Move the object 1 unit along the X-axis
```

Rotation in Three.js

Rotations are applied relative to the object's axes. In Three.js, rotation values are in radians.

object.rotation.y += Math.PI / 2; *// Rotate the object 90 degrees around the Y-axis*

Scaling Objects

Scaling an object changes its size along the three axes.

object.scale.set(2, 2, 2); *// Scale the object to twice its original size*

World vs. Local Space

It's important to understand the difference between world and local space:

- **World Space**: Coordinates relative to the global origin of the scene.
- **Local Space**: Coordinates relative to the object's origin.

Hierarchical Transformations

In a parent-child relationship, transformations on the parent affect the child. This is crucial for creating complex 3D structures.

Viewing Transformations in Action

Experiment with these transformations to understand how they affect objects. You can start by creating simple shapes and applying different transformations to see the results.

Using Helpers for Visualization

Three.js provides helper objects like AxesHelper to visualize transformations and coordinate systems.

const axesHelper = **new** THREE.AxesHelper(5);

```
scene.add(axesHelper);
```

Conclusion

Understanding the 3D coordinate system and basic transformations is critical for 3D graphics development in Three.js. Mastery of these concepts allows you to position, orient, and scale objects precisely in your 3D scenes, forming the foundation for more complex 3D modeling and animation techniques that will be covered in subsequent sections.

2.2. Basics of Geometry and Meshes

In Three.js, as in any 3D graphics programming, geometry and meshes form the building blocks of your 3D scene. Understanding these concepts is key to creating any 3D object.

Understanding Geometry in Three.js

Geometry in Three.js represents the shape or structure of a 3D object. It is defined by a collection of points (vertices) and lines (edges) that form the object's surface.

Creating Basic Geometries

Three.js provides several basic geometries like boxes, spheres, cylinders, and more. For example, creating a box geometry:

```
const geometry = new THREE.BoxGeometry(1, 1, 1);
```

Vertices and Faces

- **Vertices**: The corners or points of the geometry.

- **Faces**: Triangular areas defined by connecting three vertices.

Meshes: Combining Geometry with Material

A mesh in Three.js is an object that combines geometry with material. It is what you finally see rendered in the 3D world.

Creating a Mesh

To create a mesh, you need geometry and material:

```
const material = new THREE.MeshBasicMaterial({ color: 0xff0000 });

const cube = new THREE.Mesh(geometry, material);

scene.add(cube);
```

Understanding Materials

Materials define the appearance of your geometry — its color, how it reflects light, and more. There are several types of materials in Three.js, each with its own properties and uses.

Basic Material Types

- **MeshBasicMaterial**: A simple material that is not affected by lights.

- **MeshLambertMaterial**: A material that reacts to light, giving a flat-shaded look.

- **MeshPhongMaterial**: Similar to Lambert but with shiny surfaces.

Wireframe Mode

To better understand the structure of your geometry, you can display it in wireframe mode:

```
const wireframeMaterial = new THREE.MeshBasicMaterial({ color: 0x00ff00, wireframe: true });

const wireframeCube = new THREE.Mesh(geometry, wireframeMaterial);

scene.add(wireframeCube);
```

Custom Geometries

Beyond the basic shapes, you can create custom geometries by defining your own vertices and faces:

```
const customGeometry = new THREE.Geometry();

customGeometry.vertices.push(new THREE.Vector3(0, 0, 0));

customGeometry.vertices.push(new THREE.Vector3(0, 1, 0));

customGeometry.vertices.push(new THREE.Vector3(1, 1, 0));

customGeometry.faces.push(new THREE.Face3(0, 1, 2));
```

Normals and Face Orientation

Normals are vectors perpendicular to the surface of a geometry. They are essential for correctly calculating lighting and shading.

Visualizing Normals

Three.js provides a VertexNormalsHelper to visualize the normals of a geometry.

BufferGeometry for Performance

For complex or dynamic geometries, BufferGeometry is a more efficient form of geometry that improves performance by reducing the overhead of JavaScript objects.

Updating Geometry

You can modify the vertices of a geometry to create animations or interactive objects. However, remember to update the appropriate flags to reflect these changes:

```
geometry.vertices[0].x += 0.1;

geometry.verticesNeedUpdate = true;
```

Combining Geometries

You can create complex objects by combining multiple geometries using operations like merging.

The Role of UV Mapping

UV mapping is the process of projecting a 2D image onto a 3D model. It is essential for applying textures accurately on geometries.

Conclusion

Understanding the basics of geometry and meshes is crucial in 3D graphics creation with Three.js. By mastering these foundational elements, you are now equipped to start building more complex and visually interesting 3D scenes. In the upcoming sections, we will delve deeper into more advanced aspects of geometry, textures, and how to bring your 3D creations to life with lighting and materials.

2.3. Lighting and Materials in 3D Space

In Three.js, lighting and materials are crucial elements that add realism and depth to your 3D scenes. This section explores the various types of lights and materials available in Three.js and how they interact to create the desired visual effects.

Understanding the Role of Lighting

Lighting in 3D graphics is more than just making things visible; it's about creating mood, depth, and realism. The way light interacts with materials fundamentally affects the appearance of your scene.

Types of Lights in Three.js

- **Ambient Light**: A light that globally illuminates all objects in the scene equally, without casting shadows.
- **Point Light**: A light that emits from a single point in all directions, like a light bulb.
- **Directional Light**: A light that acts like the sun, emitting parallel light rays.
- **Spot Light**: A light that emits from a source and spreads outward in a cone.

Creating and Adding Lights

To add lighting to your scene, create a light object and add it to your scene:

```
const pointLight = new THREE.PointLight(0xffffff, 1, 100);

pointLight.position.set(10, 10, 10);
```

scene.add(pointLight);

The Impact of Materials

Materials define how the surface of your geometries interacts with light. The choice of material affects how light reflects, refracts, or gets absorbed.

Basic Material Properties

- **Color**: The base color or texture of the material.
- **Emissiveness**: How much light the material emits on its own.
- **Specularity**: How shiny the material appears.

Different Types of Materials

- **MeshBasicMaterial**: Not affected by lights, good for unlit scenes.
- **MeshLambertMaterial**: Reacts to lighting, ideal for non-shiny surfaces.
- **MeshPhongMaterial**: Reacts to lighting with a shiny surface, good for metallic or glossy surfaces.

Adding Materials to Geometries

Create a material and apply it to a geometry to create a mesh:

const material = **new** THREE.MeshPhongMaterial({ color: 0x00ff00 });

const cube = **new** THREE.Mesh(geometry, material);

```
scene.add(cube);
```

Understanding Shading Models

Shading models determine how light and material interact:

- **Flat Shading**: Each face of the geometry is a single color.
- **Smooth Shading**: Colors are interpolated between faces, giving a smooth appearance.

Casting and Receiving Shadows

For more realism, you can enable shadows in your scene:

```
renderer.shadowMap.enabled = true;

light.castShadow = true;

object.receiveShadow = true;
```

Light Attenuation

Attenuation is the decrease in light intensity over distance. Point lights and spotlights in Three.js can simulate this effect.

Using Light Helpers

Three.js provides helper objects like PointLightHelper to visualize and debug the position and effect of lights.

Textures in Materials

Applying textures to materials can greatly enhance the realism of your scene. Textures are 2D images mapped onto the surface of 3D objects.

const texture = **new** THREE.TextureLoader().load('textures/wood.jpg');

const texturedMaterial = **new** THREE.MeshPhongMaterial({ map: texture });

Transparency and Blending

Materials can be made transparent or blended with other materials for effects like glass or ghost-like appearances.

Custom Shader Materials

For advanced users, Three.js allows the creation of custom shaders, enabling highly detailed and unique material effects.

Performance Considerations

While lights and materials add realism, they also require more computational power. Balance the visual quality with performance for the best user experience.

Conclusion

Lighting and materials are essential for creating visually compelling 3D scenes in Three.js. By understanding and utilizing the various types of lights and materials, you can create a range of effects from realistic to stylized looks. In the next sections, we will explore advanced topics in geometry, textures, and lighting techniques to further enhance your 3D graphics skills.

2.4. Cameras and Perspectives

Cameras in Three.js are akin to cameras in the real world. They are the viewer's eye in the 3D space, and understanding how to manipulate them is key to creating compelling 3D scenes. This section covers the different types of cameras in Three.js and how to use them effectively.

The Role of Cameras in Three.js

In Three.js, the camera determines what part of the 3D scene is visible and how it is projected onto the 2D screen.

PerspectiveCamera

The PerspectiveCamera is the most commonly used camera in Three.js. It mimics human vision, creating a sense of depth and perspective.

```
const camera = new THREE.PerspectiveCamera(75, window.innerWidth / window.innerHeight, 0.1, 1000);

camera.position.z = 5;
```

OrthographicCamera

The OrthographicCamera provides a 2D projection, where objects are the same size regardless of their distance from the camera. This is useful for games or technical applications.

```
const camera = new THREE.OrthographicCamera(width / -2, width / 2, height / 2, height / -2, 1, 1000);

camera.position.z = 5;
```

Camera Properties

- **Field of View:** In PerspectiveCamera, it determines the extent of the scene visible on the display at any moment.

- **Aspect Ratio**: The ratio of the width to the height of the scene. It's typically the canvas width divided by its height.
- **Near and Far Clipping Planes**: These planes determine how close or far away an object can be from the camera to be rendered.

Positioning and Moving the Camera

You can move the camera in the 3D space just like any other object:

```
camera.position.set(10, 10, 10);

camera.lookAt(scene.position);
```

Using Camera Controls

Three.js offers several controls to interact with the camera:

- **OrbitControls**: Lets the camera orbit around a target point.
- **TrackballControls**: Similar to OrbitControls but with additional features like panning.
- **FirstPersonControls**: Mimics the first-person perspective, useful in games.

```
const controls = new THREE.OrbitControls(camera, renderer.domElement);
```

View Frustum

The view frustum in perspective projection is a truncated pyramid that defines the visible space. Objects outside this frustum are not rendered.

Camera Types for Different Applications

The choice of camera depends on the type of application:

- **Dynamic, Interactive Scenes**: PerspectiveCamera with OrbitControls.
- **Architectural Visualization**: OrthographicCamera for accurate scale representation.
- **First-Person Games**: PerspectiveCamera with FirstPersonControls.

Animating Cameras

You can animate cameras to move or focus on different parts of the scene:

```
function animate() {

requestAnimationFrame(animate);

camera.position.x += 0.05;

renderer.render(scene, camera);

}
```

Multiple Cameras

In complex scenes, you might use multiple cameras and switch between them for different views.

Camera Helpers

Three.js provides helpers like CameraHelper to visualize the frustum of a camera, aiding in debugging and setting up the scene.

Handling Aspect Ratio Changes

Respond to window resize events to adjust the camera's aspect ratio:

```
window.addEventListener('resize', () => {

camera.aspect = window.innerWidth / window.innerHeight;

camera.updateProjectionMatrix();

renderer.setSize(window.innerWidth, window.innerHeight);

});
```

Depth of Field and Post-Processing

Advanced effects like depth of field can be achieved using post-processing techniques in Three.js.

Conclusion

Cameras are a vital component in Three.js, determining how the 3D world is captured and presented to the user. Understanding different types of cameras and how to manipulate them is essential for creating dynamic and immersive 3D experiences. The next sections will delve deeper into rendering techniques, bringing scenes to life with animation and interactivity.

2.5. Rendering Loops: Bringing Scenes to Life

In Three.js, the rendering loop is the heartbeat of any animation or interactive element in your 3D scene. This section explores how to create and manage rendering loops effectively to animate objects, control interactivity, and ensure smooth performance.

The Concept of a Rendering Loop

A rendering loop in Three.js is a continuous cycle that updates and renders your scene. It is the core of any animation, constantly refreshing the scene to reflect changes in real time.

Basic Structure of a Rendering Loop

The basic structure of a rendering loop involves requesting the next frame and then rendering the scene:

```
function animate() {

requestAnimationFrame(animate);

renderer.render(scene, camera);

}

animate();
```

Using requestAnimationFrame

requestAnimationFrame is a JavaScript method that tells the browser you wish to perform an animation. It requests the browser to call a specified function before the next repaint.

Advantages of requestAnimationFrame

- **Efficiency**: It's optimized for animations, reducing CPU and GPU usage when the tab is not active.

- **Smooth Animations**: Syncs with the browser's refresh rate for smoother animations.

Animating Objects

To animate an object, update its properties within the loop:

```
function animate() {
requestAnimationFrame(animate);
cube.rotation.x += 0.01;
cube.rotation.y += 0.01;
renderer.render(scene, camera);
}
```

Managing Animation Speed

Control the speed of animations using time deltas or external libraries for more complex timing.

Example with Time Delta

```
let lastTime = 0;
function animate(time) {
requestAnimationFrame(animate);
let deltaTime = time - lastTime;
lastTime = time;
cube.rotation.x += deltaTime * 0.001;
renderer.render(scene, camera);
}
```

```
animate();
```

Interactive Animations

To create interactive animations, integrate event listeners in your render loop, responding to user inputs like mouse movements or clicks.

Handling Window Resizing

Adjust your camera and renderer when the browser window resizes to maintain the correct aspect ratio and prevent stretching:

```
window.addEventListener('resize', onWindowResize, false);

function onWindowResize() {

camera.aspect = window.innerWidth / window.innerHeight;

camera.updateProjectionMatrix();

renderer.setSize(window.innerWidth, window.innerHeight);

}
```

Performance Optimization

Rendering loops can be demanding on system resources. Optimize performance by:

- **Minimizing Complex Calculations**: Reduce the complexity of calculations within the loop.

- **Using LOD (Level of Detail)**: Implement different levels of detail for objects based on their distance from the camera.

Conditional Rendering

In some cases, you might not need to re-render the scene every frame. Use conditions to render only when necessary.

Debugging Rendering Issues

Use tools like the Three.js inspector and browser developer tools to debug and profile your rendering loop.

Pausing and Resuming the Loop

Provide functionality to pause and resume the rendering loop, which is especially useful in interactive applications.

Integrating Physics

For simulations or games, integrate a physics engine into your rendering loop for realistic movements and collisions.

Rendering Multiple Scenes

Advanced scenarios might require rendering multiple scenes in a single loop, each with its own camera and settings.

Conclusion

The rendering loop is a critical component in Three.js, driving animations and interactivity in your 3D scenes. Understanding how to set up and manage these loops efficiently is key to creating engaging and performant 3D applications. The following chapters will build upon these concepts, introducing more advanced techniques and tools for creating dynamic and interactive 3D content.

Chapter 3: Advanced Geometry and Textures

3.1. Creating Complex 3D Models

In Three.js, creating complex 3D models is a step up from using basic geometries. This section delves into the techniques and tools needed to build, import, and manipulate complex 3D models, enhancing the visual appeal and realism of your scenes.

The Leap to Complex Models

Transitioning from simple shapes to complex models involves understanding advanced geometries, the use of external tools, and integrating models into Three.js.

Why Complex Models?

Complex models are essential for creating detailed and lifelike 3D scenes. They can represent realistic objects, characters, and environments.

Understanding Advanced Geometries

Advanced geometries in Three.js go beyond basic shapes, allowing for the creation of intricate and detailed models.

Parametric Geometries

Three.js includes parametric geometries that can be customized with parameters, offering more control and flexibility.

Example: TorusKnotGeometry

```
const geometry = new THREE.TorusKnotGeometry(10, 3, 100, 16);

const material = new THREE.MeshBasicMaterial({ color: 0xffff00 });

const torusKnot = new THREE.Mesh(geometry, material);

scene.add(torusKnot);
```

Using 3D Modeling Software

For highly detailed models, 3D modeling software like Blender, Maya, or 3ds Max is used. These models are then exported to a format compatible with Three.js, such as GLTF or FBX.

The Workflow

1. **Model Creation**: Use 3D modeling software to create your detailed model.
2. **Texturing and Lighting**: Apply textures and set up lighting in the software.
3. **Exporting**: Export the model in a Three.js-compatible format.

Importing Models into Three.js

Three.js provides loaders for various formats. The GLTFLoader is commonly used for its efficiency and support for complex models.

Example: Loading a GLTF Model

```
const loader = new THREE.GLTFLoader();
loader.load('path/to/model.gltf', function(gltf) {
scene.add(gltf.scene);
});
```

Manipulating Imported Models

Once loaded, you can manipulate these models like any other object in Three.js — scaling, rotating, or applying animations.

Creating Models Programmatically

For unique or procedural models, you can create geometries programmatically in Three.js.

Example: Custom Geometry

```
const customGeometry = new THREE.BufferGeometry();
// Define vertices and faces here
const customMesh = new THREE.Mesh(customGeometry, material);
scene.add(customMesh);
```

Using Subdivision Surfaces

Subdivision surface modifiers can smooth and enhance the appearance of geometries, making them look more organic.

Texture Mapping on Complex Models

Textures play a crucial role in giving models a realistic appearance. Three.js supports various texture mapping techniques to apply images, patterns, and details to models.

UV Mapping

Proper UV mapping in the 3D modeling software ensures textures are correctly applied to the model in Three.js.

Normal Maps and Displacement Maps

Normal and displacement maps add detail and depth to models without increasing the number of polygons.

Interactive Complex Models

Adding interactivity to complex models can involve animations, physics, and user input handling.

Performance Considerations

Complex models are resource-intensive. Optimize performance by:

- **Reducing Polygon Count**: Simplify models without significantly affecting visual quality.

- **Level of Detail (LOD)**: Use different model resolutions based on the camera distance.

Conclusion

Creating complex 3D models in Three.js involves a combination of 3D modeling skills, understanding advanced geometries, and efficient use of textures and materials. Whether you're importing models from external software or building them programmatically, mastering these techniques will elevate the quality and realism of your 3D scenes. The following sections will explore textures in more detail, as well as techniques for mapping and optimizing them for web environments.

3.2. Applying Textures to Objects

Textures are crucial in Three.js for adding realism and detail to 3D objects. This section explores how to apply and manipulate textures, enhancing the visual quality of your models.

Understanding Textures in Three.js

A texture in Three.js is essentially an image that is mapped onto the surface of a geometry. It can represent details like color, roughness, or even bumps.

The TextureLoader Class

To load a texture, Three.js provides the TextureLoader class:

```
const loader = new THREE.TextureLoader();

const texture = loader.load('path/to/texture.jpg');
```

Applying a Texture to a Material

Once loaded, a texture can be applied to the material of an object:

```
const material = new THREE.MeshBasicMaterial({ map: texture
});

const cube = new THREE.Mesh(geometry, material);
```

scene.add(cube);

Texture Mapping Techniques

- **UV Mapping**: The most common method where the 2D texture is wrapped onto the 3D model based on UV coordinates.
- **Projection Mapping**: Projecting a texture onto an object like a slide projector.

Handling Texture Loading

Since textures are loaded asynchronously, it's important to handle the loading process correctly, often using callbacks or promises.

Example with Loading Manager

```
const manager = new THREE.LoadingManager();

const texture = new THREE.TextureLoader(manager).load('path/to/texture.jpg');
```

Repeating Textures

Textures can be repeated across a surface to create patterns:

```
texture.wrapS = THREE.RepeatWrapping;

texture.wrapT = THREE.RepeatWrapping;

texture.repeat.set(4, 4);
```

Texture Filtering

Filtering affects how textures are displayed, especially when viewed from a distance or at an angle:

- **Nearest Filter**: Pixelated look, as it uses the nearest pixel's color.
- **Linear Filter**: Smooths the texture by averaging the colors of nearby pixels.

Mipmapping for Performance

Mipmaps are smaller versions of a texture that are used when the texture is far away or at a steep angle, improving performance.

Texture Anisotropy

Anisotropy makes textures look better at glancing angles. It's a property of the renderer:

```
texture.anisotropy = renderer.capabilities.getMaxAnisotropy();
```

Using Multiple Textures

Objects can have multiple textures, like a color map, bump map, and specular map, to create more detailed and realistic surfaces.

Dynamic Textures

Textures can be dynamic, updated in real-time, for effects like video textures or interactive surfaces.

Example: Video Texture

```
const video = document.createElement('video');
```

```
// Set up video properties

const videoTexture = new THREE.VideoTexture(video);
```

Transparency in Textures

Textures can include an alpha channel to create transparent areas on a material.

Environment Mapping

Environment maps allow objects to reflect or refract their surroundings, creating effects like glass or metal.

Texture Optimization

For web applications, optimize texture size and format to balance quality and performance.

Conclusion

Applying and manipulating textures in Three.js is a powerful way to enhance the realism and visual appeal of your 3D objects. Proper use of textures, combined with the right mapping and filtering techniques, can significantly improve the appearance of your scene. The next sections will delve deeper into advanced texturing techniques, UV mapping, and how to use these tools to create more immersive and engaging 3D experiences.

3.3. UV Mapping Explained

UV mapping is a critical process in 3D modeling and rendering, allowing for detailed and accurate texturing of 3D models. This section covers the basics of UV mapping, its importance in Three.js, and how to apply it effectively.

Understanding UV Mapping

UV mapping is the technique of projecting a 2D image (texture) onto a 3D model. The 'U' and 'V' refer to the axes of the 2D texture space, analogous to the X and Y axes in 3D space.

Why UV Mapping is Important

UV mapping ensures that textures are correctly applied to the surfaces of 3D objects, allowing for detailed and realistic rendering.

The UV Mapping Process

1. **Creating UV Layouts**: This involves unwrapping the 3D model into a 2D representation.
2. **Editing UVs**: Adjusting the UV layout to minimize distortion and maximize texture space utilization.
3. **Applying Textures**: Using the UV layout to apply textures on the 3D model.

UV Mapping in 3D Modeling Software

Most UV mapping is done in 3D modeling software like Blender, Maya, or 3ds Max, where you have tools to create and edit UV layouts.

Example: UV Mapping in Blender

- Import or create a 3D model.
- Use the UV editing tools to unwrap the model and adjust the UVs.
- Export the model with the UV layout for use in Three.js.

Exporting Models with UV Maps

When exporting your model from 3D software, ensure that the UV map is included. Formats like FBX and GLTF support embedded UV maps.

Loading UV-Mapped Models in Three.js

Once exported, use Three.js loaders to import the model. The UV mapping should be automatically applied if included in the model file.

```
const loader = new THREE.GLTFLoader();

loader.load('path/to/uv-mapped-model.gltf', function(gltf) {

scene.add(gltf.scene);

});
```

Texturing UV-Mapped Models

Apply textures to the model in Three.js by assigning them to the material. The UV map guides how the texture wraps the model.

```
const texture = new THREE.TextureLoader().load('path/to/texture.jpg');

const material = new THREE.MeshBasicMaterial({ map: texture });
```

Troubleshooting UV Mapping Issues

Common issues with UV mapping include stretching, distortion, and seams. These are usually fixed in the 3D modeling software by adjusting the UV layout.

Creating UV Maps for Complex Models

For complex models, creating an efficient UV map can be challenging. It often requires breaking the model into smaller parts and unwrapping them individually.

Using Multiple UV Maps

Some advanced applications may require multiple UV maps on a single model, such as for lightmaps or detail textures.

UV Mapping for Performance

Optimize your UV maps for performance by minimizing texture size and maximizing space utilization in the texture.

Dynamic UV Mapping

In advanced scenarios, UV coordinates can be manipulated in real-time in Three.js for dynamic texturing effects.

Conclusion

UV mapping is a vital skill in the realm of 3D graphics, essential for applying textures accurately and effectively to 3D models. While most of the heavy lifting is done in 3D modeling software, understanding how UV maps work and how to apply them in Three.js is crucial for any 3D web developer. The next sections will build upon this knowledge, exploring more advanced texturing techniques and their applications in Three.js.

3.4. Importing and Using External 3D Models

In the world of Three.js, the ability to import and use external 3D models is a game-changer, opening up a realm of possibilities for creating rich and complex scenes. This section covers the essentials of importing various 3D model formats and integrating them into your Three.js projects.

Why Import External Models?

Creating models within Three.js can be limiting for complex shapes and detailed designs. Using external 3D modeling software allows for more intricate and realistic models, which can then be imported into Three.js.

Supported Model Formats in Three.js

Three.js supports several formats for 3D models, including:

- **GLTF (GL Transmission Format)**: Recommended for its efficiency and versatility.
- **FBX**: Widely used in the industry, especially for complex animations.
- **OBJ**: A simple format for static models without animations.

Using the GLTFLoader

The GLTFLoader is the most common loader for importing models in the GLTF format:

```
const loader = new THREE.GLTFLoader();
```

```
loader.load('path/to/model.gltf', function(gltf) {
scene.add(gltf.scene);
});
```

Importing FBX Models

For FBX models, especially those with animations, use the FBXLoader:

```
const loader = new THREE.FBXLoader();
loader.load('path/to/model.fbx', function(fbx) {
scene.add(fbx);
});
```

Managing Scale and Orientation

Often, imported models need to be scaled or oriented to fit correctly in your Three.js scene:

```
model.scale.set(0.1, 0.1, 0.1);
model.rotation.y = Math.PI; // Rotate 180 degrees
```

Handling Textures and Materials

If your model comes with textures and materials, the loaders will typically handle them. However, you may need to adjust material properties to achieve the desired appearance in Three.js:

```
model.traverse(function(child) {
if (child.isMesh) {
```

```
child.material.side = THREE.DoubleSide;
}
});
```

Importing Animations

Many model formats support animations. When importing these models, use the appropriate loader and methods to access and play animations:

```
const mixer = new THREE.AnimationMixer(model);
const action = mixer.clipAction(gltf.animations[0]);
action.play();
```

Optimizing Model Performance

Large or complex models can impact performance. Optimize them by reducing polygon count, compressing textures, and using level of detail (LOD).

Using Loading Managers

For better control over the loading process, especially when loading multiple models or assets, use the LoadingManager:

```
const manager = new THREE.LoadingManager();
manager.onLoad = function() {
console.log('All assets loaded');
};
// Load models using this manager
```

Handling Asynchronous Loading

Since model loading is asynchronous, ensure that your scene rendering or user interactions account for this. You can use loading indicators or callbacks to manage this.

Working with Physics and Collisions

If your scene involves physics or collision detection, you'll need to set up corresponding physics bodies for your imported models, matching their shapes and sizes.

Integrating External Models with Custom Code

Once imported, these models can interact with other objects, lights, and animations you've defined in your Three.js code.

Creating Interactive Scenes

Imported models can be part of interactive scenes, responding to user inputs, participating in animations, or being part of game logic.

Conclusion

Importing and using external 3D models in Three.js greatly enhances the visual quality and possibilities of your 3D scenes. By mastering the import process, handling different file formats, and optimizing for performance, you can create rich, interactive, and immersive 3D experiences. The next sections will explore further into procedural geometry generation and how to dynamically create complex models within Three.js.

3.5. Procedural Geometry Generation

Procedural geometry generation in Three.js allows for the dynamic creation of complex shapes and patterns. This section explores the principles and techniques of procedural geometry generation and how to implement them in your Three.js projects.

Understanding Procedural Geometry

Procedural geometry involves creating 3D shapes and structures algorithmically, as opposed to modeling them by hand. This approach is powerful for generating complex, detailed, and often random or organic structures.

Benefits of Procedural Generation

- **Flexibility**: Easily create a wide variety of shapes and patterns.
- **Efficiency**: Generate complex structures with less code and fewer resources.
- **Dynamism**: Create interactive and evolving geometries in real time.

Basic Concepts in Procedural Generation

- **Algorithmic Patterns**: Use mathematical formulas and algorithms to define the shape and structure of the geometry.
- **Randomness**: Introduce randomness for natural-looking variations.

- **Noise Functions**: Utilize noise functions like Perlin or Simplex noise for organic and natural patterns.

Creating a Simple Procedural Geometry

Start with a basic shape and modify its vertices according to some algorithmic rule:

```
const geometry = new THREE.BoxGeometry();

for (let i = 0; i < geometry.vertices.length; i++) {

geometry.vertices[i].x += Math.random() - 0.5;

}
```

Noise-Based Geometries

Use noise functions to create more complex and organic shapes:

```
const geometry = new THREE.PlaneGeometry(100, 100, 100, 100);

const noise = new SimplexNoise();

for (let i = 0; i < geometry.vertices.length; i++) {

geometry.vertices[i].z = noise.noise(geometry.vertices[i].x * 0.1, geometry.vertices[i].y * 0.1);

}
```

Fractal Geometries

Fractals are shapes that repeat their structure at different scales, and they can be created procedurally:

```
function createFractalGeometry(baseGeometry, iterations) {
```

```
let geometry = baseGeometry;

for (let i = 0; i < iterations; i++) {

// Modify geometry here

}

return geometry;

}
```

Parametric Surfaces

Create surfaces where the position of each point is defined by a parametric function:

```
const parametricFunction = (u, v, target) => {

target.set(

Math.sin(u) * 10,

Math.sin(v) * 10,

Math.sin(u + v) * 10

);

};

const geometry = new THREE.ParametricGeometry(parametricFunction, 100, 100);
```

Procedural Terrain Generation

Generate landscapes or terrains using noise functions and height maps:

```
const terrainGeometry = new THREE.PlaneGeometry(200, 200, 50, 50);

// Apply noise-based height modifications here
```

Creating Procedural Trees and Plants

Use recursive algorithms to create trees, plants, and other natural structures.

Dynamic Geometry Changes

Procedural geometries can be dynamically updated in the render loop for animations or interactive effects.

Performance Considerations

Procedural generation can be computationally intensive. Optimize by limiting the number of vertices and using efficient algorithms.

Combining with Materials and Textures

Enhance the appearance of procedural geometries with suitable materials and textures. For example, applying a bark texture to a procedurally generated tree.

Procedural Geometry in Interactive Applications

In interactive applications, procedural geometries can be used to create dynamic environments that respond to user input or game events.

Advanced Techniques

Explore advanced procedural generation techniques like L-systems for more complex structures and patterns.

Conclusion

Procedural geometry generation in Three.js opens up a vast array of possibilities for creating dynamic and intricate 3D models and environments. By mastering these techniques, you can add a new level of depth and interactivity to your 3D projects, pushing the boundaries of what can be achieved in web-based 3D graphics. The next chapters will delve into lighting and shadow techniques, further enhancing the realism and visual appeal of your procedural creations.

Chapter 4: Lighting and Shadows

4.1. Types of Lights in Three.js

Lighting plays a critical role in 3D graphics, adding depth, atmosphere, and realism to scenes. This section will explore the various types of lights available in Three.js, their characteristics, and how to use them effectively in your projects.

The Role of Lighting in Three.js

In Three.js, lights are essential for illuminating the objects in a scene and creating the desired mood and ambiance. Different types of lights can be used to achieve various effects.

Ambient Light

- **Characteristics**: Illuminates all objects in the scene equally.
- **Use Cases**: To provide overall illumination without shadows.
- **Implementation**:

```
const ambientLight = new THREE.AmbientLight(0xffffff, 0.5);
scene.add(ambientLight);
```

Point Light

- **Characteristics**: Emits light in all directions from a single point.

• **Use Cases**: To simulate light sources like bulbs or candles.

• **Implementation**:

```
const pointLight = new THREE.PointLight(0xffffff, 1, 100);

pointLight.position.set(10, 10, 10);

scene.add(pointLight);
```

Directional Light

• **Characteristics**: Emulates sunlight, casting parallel light rays.

• **Use Cases**: For outdoor scenes, simulating sunlight.

• **Implementation**:

```
const directionalLight = new THREE.DirectionalLight(0xffffff, 1);

directionalLight.position.set(0, 10, 0);

scene.add(directionalLight);
```

Spotlight

• **Characteristics**: Shines light in a specific direction, with a cone-shaped beam.

• **Use Cases**: For focused illumination, like stage lights.

• **Implementation**:

```
const spotLight = new THREE.SpotLight(0xffffff, 1);

spotLight.position.set(15, 40, 35);

scene.add(spotLight);
```

Hemisphere Light

- **Characteristics**: Simulates the effect of a bright sky and dark ground.
- **Use Cases**: For creating a natural outdoor light environment.
- **Implementation**:

```
const hemiLight = new THREE.HemisphereLight(0xffffbb, 0x080820, 1);

scene.add(hemiLight);
```

Area Light (Not Native to Three.js)

- **Characteristics**: Emits light within a defined rectangular area.
- **Use Cases**: For soft, diffused lighting like window light.
- **Note**: Requires additional libraries or custom shaders in Three.js.

Understanding Light Properties

- **Color**: Defines the color of the light.
- **Intensity**: Controls how strong the light is.

• **Distance**: For point and spotlights, defines the range of the light.

Casting Shadows

• To enable shadows, set castShadow on the light and receiveShadow on the objects.

• Consider the performance impact of shadows, especially in complex scenes.

Light Helpers

• Three.js provides helpers like SpotLightHelper to visualize the position and direction of lights, aiding in debugging and setup.

• Example:

```
const helper = new THREE.SpotLightHelper(spotLight);

scene.add(helper);
```

Animating Lights

• Lights can be animated like any other object in Three.js, changing position, color, and intensity over time.

Performance Considerations

• More lights and shadows can significantly impact performance. Optimize by limiting the number of lights and using baked lighting for static scenes.

Conclusion

Understanding and utilizing the different types of lights in Three.js is crucial for setting the mood and enhancing the visual quality of your 3D scenes. By carefully selecting and configuring lights, you can create a wide range of atmospheres and effects, from dramatic and moody to bright and cheerful. The following sections will delve deeper into techniques for realistic lighting, shadow mapping, and performance considerations.

4.2. Techniques for Realistic Lighting

Creating realistic lighting in Three.js involves more than just placing lights in a scene. It requires an understanding of how light behaves in the real world and how to replicate these effects using Three.js's lighting system. This section covers various techniques to achieve more realistic lighting in your 3D scenes.

Understanding Real-World Lighting

- Real-world lighting is complex, involving direct light, indirect light, reflections, and refractions.

- The goal in Three.js is to simulate these effects to enhance realism.

Using Physical Light Properties

- Set light properties in Three.js to mimic real-world lights, like intensity, color temperature, and falloff.

- Example of a realistic point light:

```
const pointLight = new THREE.PointLight(0xffaa00, 1, 100);

pointLight.decay = 2;

pointLight.distance = 50;

scene.add(pointLight);
```

Soft Shadows for Realism

- Soft shadows are more realistic than hard-edged shadows.
- Achieve soft shadows by adjusting the light's shadow map parameters:

```
light.shadow.mapSize.width = 1024;

light.shadow.mapSize.height = 1024;

light.shadow.radius = 10;
```

Using Ambient Occlusion

- Ambient occlusion adds depth to scenes by simulating how light behaves in corners and crevices.
- Implement ambient occlusion in Three.js using post-processing techniques like SSAO (Screen Space Ambient Occlusion).

Image-Based Lighting (IBL)

- IBL uses a surrounding environment map to provide realistic lighting and reflections.

• Example of setting an environment map:

```
const envMap = new THREE.CubeTextureLoader().load(['px.jpg', 'nx.jpg', 'py.jpg', 'ny.jpg', 'pz.jpg', 'nz.jpg']);

scene.environment = envMap;
```

HDR Lighting

• High Dynamic Range (HDR) lighting allows for a more realistic range of light intensities.

• Use HDR environment maps for more dynamic and impactful lighting.

Realistic Materials

• The realism of lighting is greatly affected by the materials used. Use physically based rendering (PBR) materials for better interaction with light.

• Example of a PBR material:

```
const pbrMaterial = new THREE.MeshStandardMaterial({ color: 0x808080, metalness: 0.5, roughness: 0.5 });
```

Light Probes for Indirect Lighting

• Light probes capture and simulate indirect light in a scene.

• They are especially useful for dynamic objects interacting with static light environments.

Using Gobos for Light Patterns

- Gobos are templates that create patterns with light, like window shadows or tree leaves.

- Implement gobos in Three.js using textures and shaders.

Balancing Performance and Quality

- Realistic lighting can be performance-intensive. Balance the number of lights, shadow quality, and post-processing effects according to your performance budget.

Simulating Weather and Time of Day

- Change lighting dynamically to simulate different times of day or weather conditions.

- Adjust light color, intensity, and shadows to reflect these changes.

Conclusion

Achieving realistic lighting in Three.js is a blend of technical skills and artistic vision. By understanding and applying these techniques, you can greatly enhance the visual fidelity of your 3D scenes, creating immersive and engaging experiences. The next sections will explore shadow mapping and optimization, along with advanced techniques to create atmosphere and mood with lighting.

4.3. Shadow Mapping and Optimization

Shadows add a vital layer of depth and realism to 3D scenes, but they can also be computationally intensive. This section focuses on shadow mapping techniques in Three.js and strategies for optimizing their performance.

Basics of Shadow Mapping

- Shadow mapping in Three.js involves creating a map from the light's perspective, which is then used to calculate shadows.
- It's a crucial technique for realistic lighting but needs careful management to balance performance.

Enabling Shadows in Three.js

- To use shadows, enable them on both the renderer and the lights:

```
renderer.shadowMap.enabled = true;

const light = new THREE.DirectionalLight(0xffffff, 1);

light.castShadow = true;

scene.add(light);
```

Shadow Map Resolution

- The resolution of the shadow map significantly affects both the quality and performance:

```
light.shadow.mapSize.width = 1024; // Default is 512

light.shadow.mapSize.height = 1024; // Default is 512
```

Types of Shadow Maps

• Three.js offers different shadow mapping algorithms, such as PCFSoftShadowMap and VSMShadowMap, each with its own visual and performance characteristics.

Fine-Tuning Shadow Properties

• Adjust shadow properties like bias and radius to reduce artifacts like shadow acne or moiré patterns.

Optimizing with Light Frustum

• Adjust the light's frustum to be as tight as possible around your scene to optimize shadow calculations.

```
light.shadow.camera.near = 1;

light.shadow.camera.far = 100;

light.shadow.camera.left = -50;

light.shadow.camera.right = 50;

light.shadow.camera.top = 50;

light.shadow.camera.bottom = -50;
```

Shadow Casting and Receiving

• Not all objects in the scene need to cast or receive shadows. Optimize by setting castShadow and receiveShadow appropriately:

```
object.castShadow = true;
```

```
ground.receiveShadow = true;
```

Baked Shadows

- For static scenes, consider using baked shadows. These are pre-calculated and included in the textures, reducing real-time computation.

Dynamic vs. Static Shadows

- Dynamic shadows are suitable for moving objects, but they require more processing power. Use static or baked shadows for static objects.

Shadow Optimization Techniques

- Use simpler geometries for shadow casting to reduce calculations.

- Limit the number of lights casting shadows.

- Combine real-time and baked shadows for efficiency.

Leveraging Shadow Helpers

- Three.js provides helpers like CameraHelper for visualizing shadow frustums, aiding in the optimization process.

Shadow Quality vs. Performance Trade-offs

- Higher-quality shadows increase realism but can significantly impact performance, especially in large scenes or on less powerful devices.

Advanced Shadow Techniques

- Explore advanced techniques like cascaded shadow maps for large outdoor scenes.

- Experiment with custom shaders for stylized shadow effects.

Conclusion

Effective shadow mapping and optimization are key to achieving realistic lighting in Three.js while maintaining good performance. By understanding the principles of shadow mapping and applying these optimization strategies, you can enhance the visual quality of your scenes without compromising on speed and responsiveness. The following sections will further explore creating atmosphere with lighting and performance considerations for complex lighting setups.

4.4. Creating Atmosphere with Lighting

Lighting is not just about visibility; it's a powerful tool to set the mood and atmosphere of a scene. In Three.js, various lighting techniques can be used to evoke emotions and tell a story. This section explores how to use lighting effectively to create atmosphere in your 3D scenes.

The Importance of Atmospheric Lighting

- Atmospheric lighting involves using light and shadow to create a specific mood or feeling, such as warmth, coldness, eeriness, or tranquility.

Using Color and Intensity

- The color and intensity of lights can greatly affect the mood. Warm colors (yellows, reds) create a cozy feeling, while cool colors (blues, purples) can evoke a sense of calmness or mystery.

```
const warmLight = new THREE.PointLight(0xffaa00, 1, 100);

const coolLight = new THREE.PointLight(0x00aaff, 1, 100);
```

Dynamic Lighting for Emotional Impact

- Changing lighting dynamically can reflect changes in emotion or narrative within a scene. This can be done by animating light properties over time.

Creating Depth with Contrast

- High contrast between light and dark areas can add depth and drama. Use a combination of bright lights and dark shadows to achieve this effect.

Fog for Atmospheric Depth

- Fog can add depth and a sense of mystery to a scene. Three.js provides simple fog effects that can be easily implemented:

```
scene.fog = new THREE.Fog(0x000000, 10, 100);
```

Soft Lighting for a Natural Feel

- Soft lighting can create a natural and less harsh atmosphere. Achieve this by using area lights or by softening the edges of shadows.

Highlighting Key Elements

- Use focused lighting, like spotlights, to draw attention to important elements or characters in the scene.

Ambient Lighting for Background Mood

- Ambient light provides general background lighting. Subtle changes in ambient light color can shift the overall mood of the scene.

Playing with Shadows

- Shadows are not just absences of light; they can be used creatively to add mystery or foreboding, or to create patterns that add visual interest.

Lighting for Time of Day

- Simulate different times of day by adjusting the color, angle, and intensity of lights. For example, use a low, orange light for sunset.

Realistic vs. Stylized Lighting

- Decide whether you want your scene to have a realistic feel or a more stylized, artistic look, and adjust your lighting accordingly.

Balancing Lights and Materials

- The effect of lighting is also determined by the materials in the scene. Ensure that your materials are set up to interact with the lights in a way that supports your atmospheric goals.

Lighting in Layers

- Think of lighting in layers: start with a base layer of ambient light, then add directional lights for depth, and finally use point or spotlights for highlights and accents.

Environmental Lighting

- Use environmental lighting, such as skyboxes or HDRIs, to create a sense of place and time.

Interactivity and Lighting

- In interactive scenes, consider how lighting can change in response to user actions, adding an additional layer of engagement.

Testing and Experimenting

- Experiment with different lighting setups and test them under various conditions to see how they affect the atmosphere of the scene.

Conclusion

Crafting atmosphere with lighting in Three.js is an art form. It requires a careful balance of technical knowledge and creative vision. By experimenting with different types of lights, colors, and intensities, you can create rich, emotionally resonant environments that enhance the storytelling and visual impact of your 3D scenes. The next sections will delve into performance considerations for lighting, ensuring that your scenes are not only beautiful but also run smoothly.

4.5. Performance Considerations for Lighting

In Three.js, while lighting is essential for creating realism and atmosphere, it can also be one of the most performance-intensive aspects of 3D rendering. This section provides insights into optimizing lighting for better performance without significantly compromising visual quality.

Understanding the Impact of Lighting on Performance

- Each light in a scene adds to the computational load, especially when casting shadows or interacting with materials.

Balancing Light Count and Quality

- Reduce the number of lights in the scene. Use fewer lights but with higher quality or use techniques like baking lights for static scenes.

Optimizing Shadow Rendering

- Shadows can be particularly performance-heavy. Optimize by reducing shadow resolution, limiting the shadow casting area, and using shadow maps efficiently.

```
light.shadow.mapSize.width = 512; // Lower resolution
```

```
light.shadow.camera.near = 1; // Tighten the frustum
```

Baking Lights for Static Scenes

- For scenes with no dynamic lighting, consider baking the lighting into textures. This approach can significantly reduce real-time lighting computations.

Using Ambient Light Wisely

- Ambient light is less performance-intensive than other types. Use ambient lighting to provide general illumination while using targeted lights for specific areas.

Implementing Light Probes for Dynamic Objects

- Light probes capture the lighting environment and can be used to light dynamic objects without the need for real-time lights.

Avoiding Overlapping Lights

- Minimize the overlap of light areas, as overlapping lights increase the rendering load.

LOD (Level of Detail) for Lights

- Implement LOD techniques for lights, where the detail and intensity of lighting decrease with distance.

Profiling and Monitoring Performance

- Regularly profile your scene's performance, focusing on how different lighting setups affect the frame rate and rendering times.

Using Deferred Shading

- Deferred shading can be more efficient for scenes with many lights. However, it requires a different setup and may have limitations with transparency and shadows.

Hardware and Browser Considerations

- Be aware of the limitations of your target audience's hardware and browsers. Tailor your lighting setup to provide the best balance for the majority of your users.

Adaptive Lighting Techniques

- Implement adaptive lighting techniques that adjust the lighting quality based on the current performance metrics.

Precomputed Lighting for Large Scenes

- For large and complex scenes, use precomputed lighting solutions, like lightmaps or irradiance environment maps, to reduce real-time calculations.

Utilizing HDR and Tone Mapping

- High Dynamic Range (HDR) and tone mapping can create more realistic lighting without a significant impact on performance.

Real-time vs. Baked Lighting Trade-offs

- Understand the trade-offs between real-time and baked lighting, choosing the best approach based on your scene's requirements and performance goals.

Conclusion

Effective lighting is crucial for creating visually appealing 3D scenes in Three.js, but it must be balanced with performance considerations. By applying these optimization strategies, you can achieve a good balance between visual quality and rendering performance, ensuring smooth and responsive experiences for your users. The upcoming chapters will delve into more advanced topics, including camera controls, animation, and interactive 3D scenes.

Chapter 5: Camera Controls and Animation

5.1. Exploring Different Camera Types

In Three.js, cameras are the window through which the 3D world is viewed. This section delves into the various types of cameras available in Three.js, their characteristics, and how to use them effectively to enhance your 3D scenes.

Understanding the Role of Cameras in Three.js

- Cameras in Three.js determine what is visible on the screen and from which perspective. Choosing the right type of camera is crucial for the desired presentation of your scene.

The Perspective Camera

- The most commonly used camera in Three.js, it mimics the way the human eye perceives the world, offering a natural and realistic view.

```
const perspectiveCamera = new THREE.PerspectiveCamera(75, window.innerWidth / window.innerHeight, 0.1, 1000);

perspectiveCamera.position.z = 5;
```

The Orthographic Camera

• This camera type uses parallel projection, which means objects far away are the same size as those close by. Useful for 2D games and architectural visualization.

```
const orthoCamera = new THREE.OrthographicCamera(width / -2, width / 2, height / 2, height / -2, 1, 1000);

orthoCamera.position.z = 5;
```

Camera Parameters and Properties

• Understanding camera parameters like field of view, aspect ratio, and near/far clipping planes is essential for setting up your camera correctly.

The Cinematic Camera

• For cinematic effects, Three.js offers a CinematicCamera that simulates the effects of real-world camera lenses.

The Cube Camera

• Used for environment mapping, the CubeCamera captures the scene from six different directions at the same point in space.

The Array Camera

• This camera type is useful for creating multi-viewpoint or split-screen effects.

Switching Between Cameras

- In interactive applications, you can switch between different cameras based on user interaction or other events.

Animating Cameras

- Camera animation can be used to create smooth transitions between scenes or to follow objects in the scene.

```
// Animating camera position

gsap.to(camera.position, { x: 10, y: 10, duration: 2 });
```

Understanding Camera Controls

- Camera controls like OrbitControls, TrackballControls, or FirstPersonControls enhance user interaction, allowing users to navigate the 3D world intuitively.

Implementing Custom Camera Controls

- For specific use cases, you might need to implement custom camera controls tailored to your application's needs.

Cameras and Responsive Design

- Ensure your camera and scene adapt to different screen sizes and aspect ratios for a responsive design.

Cameras in Virtual Reality (VR)

- In VR applications, camera setup differs as you need to account for user head movement and stereoscopic views.

Performance Considerations

- The choice of camera and its settings can impact performance, especially in large and complex scenes.

Debugging Camera Issues

- Use tools like CameraHelper to visualize camera frustums, which can aid in debugging and setting up your camera views.

Conclusion

Choosing and configuring the right camera type is fundamental for any Three.js project. Whether you're creating a realistic simulation, a 2D game, or an interactive VR experience, understanding the different camera options and how to control them will greatly enhance the effectiveness of your 3D scenes. The next sections will focus on implementing camera controls and animating cameras to create dynamic and engaging 3D experiences.

5.2. Implementing Camera Controls

Effective camera controls are essential for enhancing user interaction and navigation in 3D environments. This section covers the implementation of various camera control mechanisms in Three.js, enabling users to explore 3D scenes intuitively and efficiently.

The Importance of Camera Controls

• Camera controls allow users to navigate and interact with the 3D world, providing a dynamic and immersive experience.

Using OrbitControls

• OrbitControls allow the camera to orbit around a target point and are ideal for inspecting objects or environments.

```
const controls = new THREE.OrbitControls(camera, renderer.domElement);

controls.target.set(0, 0, 0);
```

Implementing FirstPersonControls

• FirstPersonControls are used for first-person view experiences, giving the user control as if they are moving within the scene.

```
const controls = new THREE.FirstPersonControls(camera, renderer.domElement);

controls.lookSpeed = 0.1;

controls.movementSpeed = 10;
```

Using TrackballControls

- TrackballControls provide a trackball interface to rotate, pan, and zoom the camera, offering a smooth and intuitive user interaction.

```
const controls = new
THREE.TrackballControls(camera,
renderer.domElement);
```

Creating Custom Camera Controls

- For specific requirements, custom camera controls can be implemented, providing tailored navigation and interaction capabilities.

Responding to User Input

- Camera controls should respond to various user inputs like mouse movements, scroll wheel, touch gestures, or keyboard inputs.

Implementing Smooth Camera Transitions

- Smooth transitions between camera positions can be achieved using animation libraries like GSAP or Three.js's tweening functionality.

```
gsap.to(camera.position, { x: 10, y: 10, z: 10, duration: 2
});
```

Limiting Camera Movement

- Setting limits on camera movement and rotation can prevent disorientation and ensure users stay within the intended area of the scene.

Camera Controls for Mobile Devices

- Implement touch-friendly controls for mobile devices, considering the limitations of touch interfaces.

Integrating Camera Controls with UI Elements

- Camera controls can be linked to UI elements like buttons or sliders for easier navigation and control.

Handling Window Resizing

- Ensure camera controls adapt to window resizing for a consistent experience across different screen sizes.

Camera Controls in VR

- In VR applications, camera controls are typically based on headset movement, but additional controls can be added for teleportation or navigation.

Collision Detection with Camera Controls

- Implement collision detection to prevent the camera from passing through objects while navigating the scene.

Performance Considerations

- Optimize camera control performance, especially for complex scenes or lower-powered devices.

User Experience and Accessibility

- Ensure camera controls are intuitive and accessible, providing a comfortable and engaging experience for all users.

Conclusion

Implementing effective camera controls in Three.js is crucial for creating interactive and user-friendly 3D environments. By offering various control mechanisms, from orbit and trackball controls to custom solutions, you can greatly enhance the usability and engagement of your 3D applications. The following sections will delve into the basics of keyframe animation, animating with physics, and synchronizing animations with user actions.

5.3. Basics of Keyframe Animation

Keyframe animation is a fundamental concept in 3D graphics, allowing for the creation of smooth and dynamic movements in Three.js. This section introduces the basics of keyframe animation and demonstrates how to implement it in your projects.

Understanding Keyframe Animation

- Keyframe animation involves defining specific values (keyframes) at certain points in time for an object's properties, and the system interpolates the values in between.

Setting Up Keyframes in Three.js

- In Three.js, keyframes are set up using the KeyframeTrack and AnimationClip objects.

Creating a Simple Animation

- Start with a basic animation, like moving an object from one point to another.

```
const positionKF = new THREE.VectorKeyframeTrack('.position', [0, 1], [0, 0, 0, 10, 0, 0]);

const clip = new THREE.AnimationClip('move', 1, [positionKF]);
```

The Animation Mixer

- The AnimationMixer is a player for animations on a particular object or group of objects.

```
const mixer = new THREE.AnimationMixer(object);

const action = mixer.clipAction(clip);

action.play();
```

Interpolating Between Keyframes

- Three.js automatically interpolates between keyframes, creating smooth transitions over time.

Looping and Timing

- Control the timing and repetition of animations using loop modes and duration settings.

Easing and Tweening

- Easing functions can be used for more natural or dramatic transitions between keyframes.

Animating Multiple Properties

- Combine different properties like position, rotation, and scale in a single animation for more complex movements.

Event-Driven Animations

- Trigger animations in response to events such as user interactions or other runtime conditions.

Synchronizing Multiple Animations

- Coordinate multiple animations to play in sync or in a sequence for coordinated effects.

Handling Animation Playback

- Control the playback of animations with start, stop, pause, and resume functionalities.

Updating the Animation in the Render Loop

- Update the animation mixer within the main render loop.

```
const clock = new THREE.Clock();

function animate() {

requestAnimationFrame(animate);

const delta = clock.getDelta();

mixer.update(delta);

renderer.render(scene, camera);

}
```

Using Animation Clips

• Create and use multiple animation clips for different animations on the same object.

Adding Keyframe Animations to Imported Models

• Apply keyframe animations to models imported from 3D software.

Performance Considerations

• Optimizing keyframe animations is important, especially when dealing with complex scenes or multiple animated objects.

Best Practices for Keyframe Animation

• Plan your animations, keep them consistent with the scene's context, and ensure they contribute to the overall user experience.

Conclusion

Keyframe animation is a powerful tool in the Three.js toolkit, enabling the creation of lifelike and engaging animations. By understanding the basics of setting up and controlling keyframe animations, you can add dynamic and interactive elements to your 3D scenes, bringing them to life. The next sections will explore more advanced animation techniques, including animating with physics and synchronizing animations with user actions.

5.4. Animating with Physics and Forces

Incorporating physics into animations adds realism and complexity to 3D scenes. This section delves into the integration of physics-based animations in Three.js, covering the basics of simulating forces, collisions, and natural motion.

The Role of Physics in Animation

- Physics-based animations use the laws of physics to determine the movement of objects, creating more realistic and dynamic interactions.

Integrating a Physics Engine

- While Three.js does not have a built-in physics engine, libraries like cannon.js or ammo.js can be integrated for physics simulations.

Basic Physics Concepts

- Understand basic physics concepts such as gravity, velocity, acceleration, and collisions to effectively implement physics-based animations.

Setting Up a Physics World

• Create a physics world parallel to your Three.js scene, where physics calculations are performed.

```
const world = new CANNON.World();

world.gravity.set(0, -9.82, 0);
```

Simulating Gravity and Forces

• Apply gravity and other forces to objects to simulate natural movements.

```
const body = new CANNON.Body({

mass: 1,

shape: new CANNON.Box(new CANNON.Vec3(1, 1, 1))

});

world.addBody(body);
```

Creating Rigid Bodies

• Correspond each Three.js object with a rigid body in the physics world for simulations like collisions and bouncing.

Handling Collisions

• Detect and respond to collisions between objects, adjusting their positions and velocities based on physical principles.

Implementing Springs and Damping

- Use springs and damping to create elastic and fluid motions, such as bouncing or swaying.

Animating with External Forces

- Apply external forces like wind or magnetism for more complex and varied animations.

Physics-based Character Movement

- Implement realistic character movement using physics for actions like walking, jumping, or falling.

Real-time Physics Interaction

- Allow real-time interaction with physics objects, like dragging, pushing, or throwing.

Syncing Physics with Three.js

- Continuously update the Three.js scene based on the state of the physics world.

```
function animate() {

requestAnimationFrame(animate);

world.step(1 / 60);

// Update Three.js objects based on physics calculations

renderer.render(scene, camera);
```

```
}
```

Performance Optimization

- Physics simulations can be performance-intensive. Optimize by simplifying collision shapes, reducing the number of calculations, and using sleep states for inactive objects.

Debugging Physics Animations

- Visualize the physics world alongside the Three.js scene to debug and fine-tune your animations.

Creating Realistic Deformations

- Simulate deformations on impact using soft body physics or morph targets.

Using Physics for Particle Systems

- Apply physics rules to particle systems for effects like smoke, fire, or explosions.

Conclusion

Animating with physics in Three.js brings an additional layer of realism and interactivity to your scenes. By understanding and applying physics principles and integrating with physics libraries, you can create compelling and lifelike animations that respond naturally to forces and collisions. The next section, 5.5, will explore synchronizing animations with user actions, enhancing the interactive capabilities of your 3D projects.

5.5. Synchronizing Animations with User Actions

Synchronizing animations with user actions in Three.js can greatly enhance interactivity and user engagement. This section covers various techniques for triggering and controlling animations in response to user inputs and interactions.

The Importance of Interactive Animations

- Interactive animations are those that respond to user inputs, such as mouse clicks, keyboard presses, or touch events, making the experience more dynamic and engaging.

Event Listeners for User Inputs

- Use event listeners to detect user actions and trigger animations.

```
document.addEventListener('click', () => {
// Trigger or modify an animation
});
```

Animating on Mouse Movement

- Create animations that respond to mouse movements, such as moving an object or changing its properties based on the cursor position.

```
document.addEventListener('mousemove', (event) => {
// Update animation based on mouse position
```

```
});
```

Keyboard Interactions

- Bind animations to keyboard events, allowing users to control aspects of the scene through key presses.

```
document.addEventListener('keydown', (event) => {
if (event.key === 'a') {
// Trigger an animation
}
});
```

Touch Events for Mobile Devices

- Handle touch events to enable animations on mobile devices, considering actions like swipes and pinches.

```
document.addEventListener('touchstart', (event) => {
// Start or modify an animation
});
```

Linking Animations to UI Elements

- Connect animations to UI controls like sliders, buttons, or toggles, allowing users to interactively control aspects of the animation.

```
document.getElementById('myButton').addEventListener('click',
() => {

// Play or pause an animation

});
```

Animating Object Properties

- Animate properties of objects like position, rotation, scale, or material attributes in response to user actions.

Synchronizing Multiple Animations

- Coordinate multiple animations to play in harmony or sequence based on user interactions.

Controlling Animation Playback

- Provide controls for users to start, stop, or pause animations, as well as adjust their speed or progress.

```
const mixer = new THREE.AnimationMixer(object);

// Play, pause, or adjust the mixer based on user input
```

Real-time Feedback Through Animation

- Use animations to give real-time feedback to users, such as highlighting objects when hovered or clicked.

Transition Effects

- Implement smooth transition effects between different animation states or scenes in response to user actions.

Physics-based Interactive Animations

- Incorporate physics in your animations for natural and realistic responses to user inputs.

User-driven Storytelling

- Create animations that progress or change based on user choices, enabling interactive storytelling or decision-driven gameplay.

Animation Blending

- Blend between animation states smoothly to avoid abrupt changes, enhancing the user experience.

Performance Considerations

- Ensure that interactive animations remain performant, especially when dealing with complex scenes or a large number of user interactions.

User Experience and Accessibility

- Design interactive animations with user experience in mind, ensuring they are intuitive and enhance, rather than hinder, the overall experience.

Conclusion

Synchronizing animations with user actions in Three.js adds an interactive and dynamic dimension to 3D scenes. By effectively using event listeners, UI elements, and real-time feedback mechanisms, you can create an engaging and responsive experience for your users. The next chapters will delve into more advanced topics, including interactive 3D scenes, working with audio and video, and exploring physics in Three.js.

Chapter 6: Interactive 3D Scenes

6.1 Event Handling in 3D Environments

In this section, we'll explore the crucial aspect of event handling in 3D environments using Three.js. Interactivity is a fundamental part of creating engaging and immersive 3D experiences on the web. Whether you're building a game, a product visualization, or an educational simulation, the ability to respond to user input is essential.

Understanding Event Handling

Event handling in Three.js is similar to working with events in traditional 2D web development but with the added dimension of 3D space. You can capture user interactions such as clicks, mouse movements, keyboard input, and even device-specific input like touch and gyroscope data.

To start with event handling, you need to understand the concept of the "raycaster." The raycaster is a tool that allows you to cast a ray from a specific point in 3D space into the scene and determine what objects, if any, intersect with that ray. This is the key to detecting interactions with 3D objects.

Mouse Interactions

One of the most common forms of interaction is mouse-based. You can detect mouse clicks and movements to provide responsive feedback to the user. Here's a basic example of how to set up a click event handler in Three.js:

```
// Create a raycaster and a mouse vector
```

```
const raycaster = new THREE.Raycaster();

const mouse = new THREE.Vector2();

// Add a click event listener to the document

document.addEventListener('click', onMouseClick);

function onMouseClick(event) {

// Calculate mouse coordinates relative to the canvas

mouse.x = (event.clientX / window.innerWidth) * 2 - 1;

mouse.y = -(event.clientY / window.innerHeight) * 2 + 1;

// Set the ray's origin and direction based on the mouse position

raycaster.setFromCamera(mouse, camera);

// Find intersections with objects in the scene

const intersects = raycaster.intersectObjects(scene.children, true);

// Check if any objects were clicked

if (intersects.length > 0) {

// Handle the click on the intersected object(s)

const clickedObject = intersects[0].object;

// Add your interaction logic here

}

}
```

This code snippet sets up a basic click event listener that detects clicks on 3D objects in the scene. When a click occurs, it calculates the intersection between the raycast and the objects and allows you to perform custom actions.

Other Interactions

In addition to mouse interactions, Three.js supports various other forms of input handling, including touch events, keyboard events, and even VR controller inputs. Depending on your project's requirements, you can implement multi-touch gestures, keyboard-controlled movements, and more.

It's important to note that effective event handling can significantly enhance the user experience in 3D environments. Whether you're building a game with complex controls or a simple product viewer, responsive interactivity is key to engaging your audience.

Remember that the specifics of event handling may vary depending on the type of interaction and the devices you're targeting. Always consider the user's input methods and design your interactions accordingly.

Conclusion

In this section, we've covered the fundamentals of event handling in 3D environments using Three.js. Understanding how to capture and respond to user interactions is essential for creating immersive and interactive 3D web applications. By using raycasting and event listeners, you can enable a wide range of interactive experiences in your Three.js projects.

6.2 Implementing User Interaction

In this section, we will dive into the practical aspects of implementing user interaction in Three.js. Interactive 3D scenes are not only about detecting events but also about responding to them effectively, creating engaging user experiences.

Controlling Object Movement

One common form of user interaction is allowing users to control the movement of objects in the 3D scene. This can be achieved by changing the position, rotation, or scale of objects based on user input. Here's a simplified example of how you can implement object movement using keyboard input:

```
// Define a variable to keep track of the object's position

const objectPosition = new THREE.Vector3(0, 0, 0);

// Add a keydown event listener to the document

document.addEventListener('keydown', onKeyDown);

function onKeyDown(event) {

switch (event.key) {

case 'ArrowUp':

objectPosition.y += 1;

break;

case 'ArrowDown':

objectPosition.y -= 1;

break;

case 'ArrowLeft':

objectPosition.x -= 1;
```

```
break;

case 'ArrowRight':

objectPosition.x += 1;

break;

}

// Update the object's position

object.position.set(objectPosition.x, objectPosition.y, objectPosition.z);

}
```

In this example, we listen for arrow key presses and update the position of an object accordingly. Depending on the key pressed, we adjust the object's position in the 3D scene.

User Interface Elements

To create a more user-friendly experience, you can integrate HTML-based user interface (UI) elements into your 3D scene. This allows users to interact with buttons, sliders, and other UI components to control the scene.

Here's a basic example of embedding HTML UI elements in your Three.js project:

```
<!—HTML code for UI elements—>

<div id="ui-container">

<button id="move-left">Move Left</button>

<button id="move-right">Move Right</button>
```

```
</div>

// JavaScript code to handle UI interactions

const moveLeftButton = document.getElementById('move-left');

const moveRightButton = document.getElementById('move-right');

moveLeftButton.addEventListener('click', () => {

// Implement your logic for moving objects left

});

moveRightButton.addEventListener('click', () => {

// Implement your logic for moving objects right

});
```

By combining HTML UI elements with Three.js, you can provide users with familiar controls to manipulate the 3D scene. This approach is especially useful for creating interactive product viewers and architectural visualizations.

Complex Interactions

Depending on your project's complexity, you may need to implement more sophisticated user interactions. This can include handling gestures, supporting multiple input devices (e.g., touch and mouse), and even creating custom control schemes for games.

For complex interactions, you can explore libraries like "THREE.OrbitControls" for camera manipulation, "Cannon.js" for physics-based interactions, or other custom solutions tailored to your specific needs.

Remember that effective user interaction design is critical to the success of your 3D web application. It's important to consider usability, feedback, and user guidance when implementing interactive elements.

Conclusion

In this section, we've explored the practical implementation of user interaction in Three.js. Whether you're controlling object movement, integrating HTML-based UI elements, or dealing with more complex interactions, user interaction design plays a crucial role in creating engaging and immersive 3D web experiences. By effectively responding to user input, you can provide users with intuitive and interactive control over your 3D scenes.

6.3 Creating Interactive 3D Interfaces

In this section, we'll delve into the creation of interactive 3D interfaces using Three.js. Building intuitive and engaging user interfaces within 3D environments can greatly enhance user experiences and open up new possibilities for your web applications.

The Importance of 3D Interfaces

3D interfaces are valuable in a variety of contexts, from 3D games and simulations to product configurators and educational applications. They allow users to directly interact with 3D objects and scenes, providing a more immersive and intuitive way to explore and manipulate digital content.

UI Elements in 3D Space

To create interactive 3D interfaces, you can place HTML-based UI elements within your Three.js scene. This enables users to interact with buttons, sliders, text inputs, and other familiar interface components while immersed in the 3D environment.

Here's an example of how you can embed HTML UI elements in your 3D scene:

```
<!—HTML code for UI elements—>
<div id="ui-container">
<button id="rotate-left">Rotate Left</button>
<button id="rotate-right">Rotate Right</button>
</div>
// JavaScript code to handle UI interactions
const rotateLeftButton = document.getElementById('rotate-left');
const rotateRightButton = document.getElementById('rotate-right');
rotateLeftButton.addEventListener('click', () => {
// Implement logic to rotate a 3D object left
});
rotateRightButton.addEventListener('click', () => {
// Implement logic to rotate a 3D object right
});
```

By combining HTML and JavaScript with Three.js, you can create interactive controls that allow users to manipulate 3D objects, change views, or trigger actions within your 3D scene.

Gestures and Interactions

In addition to traditional UI elements, you can implement gesture-based interactions within your 3D environment. This includes pinch-to-zoom, swipe gestures, and multi-touch gestures for scaling, rotating, and panning 3D objects.

To handle touch and gesture events, you can use libraries like Hammer.js or build custom event handlers in JavaScript to detect and respond to user input.

Spatial User Interfaces

Spatial user interfaces take advantage of 3D space to create unique interaction paradigms. For example, you can implement hand-tracking interfaces for virtual reality (VR) applications, allowing users to interact with 3D objects using their hands in a natural way. The integration of technologies like WebXR and WebVR can enable these spatial interactions.

Challenges and Considerations

While creating interactive 3D interfaces can be highly rewarding, it also comes with challenges. You must consider performance optimization, responsiveness, and accessibility. Ensure that your interfaces work well on a variety of devices and accommodate users with different input methods.

Testing and user feedback are crucial in refining your 3D interfaces. Conduct usability testing to identify any usability issues and make iterative improvements to enhance the user experience.

Conclusion

In this section, we've explored the creation of interactive 3D interfaces in Three.js. Leveraging HTML-based UI elements, gesture interactions, and spatial user interfaces, you can provide users with immersive and engaging ways to interact with 3D content. Keep in mind the importance of performance, responsiveness, and accessibility when designing and implementing these interfaces to ensure a seamless and enjoyable user experience.

6.4 Collision Detection and Response

In this section, we'll explore the concept of collision detection and response in Three.js. Collision detection is a crucial aspect of creating realistic and interactive 3D environments. It enables objects in your scene to interact with each other and respond accordingly when they collide.

The Importance of Collision Detection

Collision detection is essential for a wide range of applications, from video games and simulations to architectural visualizations and product configurators. It allows you to simulate physical interactions between objects, creating a more immersive and believable 3D experience.

Types of Collisions

In 3D environments, there are various types of collisions to consider:

1. **Object-to-Object Collision:** This occurs when two or more 3D objects intersect or come into contact with each other. It's essential for simulating interactions between characters, objects, or vehicles in a game, for example.

2. **Raycasting Collisions:** Raycasting involves sending a ray from a point in 3D space and detecting if it intersects with any objects. This is useful for things like detecting where a player is looking in a VR application or determining if a projectile hits a target.
3. **Collision with Surfaces:** Sometimes, you need to detect when an object collides with a surface, like the ground or a wall. This is crucial for physics simulations and ensuring objects don't pass through surfaces.

Implementing Collision Detection

Three.js provides tools and libraries to help you implement collision detection in your projects. Here's a simplified example of how to detect collisions between two objects:

```
// Assuming you have two objects: object1 and object2

// Create a bounding box for each object

const object1BoundingBox = new THREE.Box3().setFromObject(object1);

const object2BoundingBox = new THREE.Box3().setFromObject(object2);

// Check for intersection

const collisionDetected = object1BoundingBox.intersectsBox(object2BoundingBox);

if (collisionDetected) {

// Handle the collision
```

// You can implement custom logic here, like bouncing objects or triggering actions

}

In this example, we create bounding boxes for two objects and check if they intersect. If a collision is detected, you can implement custom logic to respond to the collision, such as changing the objects' positions or velocities.

Physics Engines

For more complex simulations and realistic physics interactions, you may consider integrating a physics engine like Cannon.js or Ammo.js with Three.js. These physics engines provide advanced collision detection and response capabilities, including support for rigid bodies, forces, and constraints.

Optimization and Performance

Efficient collision detection is critical for maintaining good performance in your 3D applications. Depending on the complexity of your scene and the number of objects, collision detection can be computationally expensive. Techniques like spatial partitioning (e.g., using Octrees) can help optimize collision checks and improve performance.

Conclusion

In this section, we've explored collision detection and response in Three.js. Understanding and implementing collision detection is essential for creating realistic and interactive 3D environments. Whether you're building a game, a simulation, or a product visualization, the ability to simulate object interactions adds depth and immersion to your projects. Be mindful of choosing the right collision detection approach for your specific use case and consider performance optimization for a smooth user experience.

6.5 Game Mechanics in Three.js

In this section, we'll delve into incorporating game mechanics into your Three.js projects. While Three.js is often used for creating interactive 3D visualizations, it can also serve as a powerful framework for developing 3D games. Game mechanics involve rules and systems that define how a game operates, and integrating them into your Three.js applications can lead to engaging and dynamic experiences.

Game Development with Three.js

Three.js provides a solid foundation for game development, offering features for 3D rendering, animation, physics, and user input handling. Here are some key components and considerations when implementing game mechanics in Three.js:

1. Game Loop: Building a game typically involves creating a game loop that updates the game's state and renders frames continuously. You can use Three.js' rendering loop in combination with your game logic.

```
function gameLoop() {

// Update game state

update();

// Render the scene

render();
```

```
// Call the game loop recursively

requestAnimationFrame(gameLoop);

}

// Start the game loop

gameLoop();
```

2. Game State: Define the various states of your game, such as the main menu, gameplay, pause menu, and game over screen. Managing and transitioning between these states is essential for creating a structured gaming experience.

3. Player Input: Handle user input, including keyboard, mouse, touch, and gamepad interactions. Three.js makes it relatively straightforward to capture and respond to user actions.

4. Physics: Integrate a physics engine like Cannon.js or Ammo.js to simulate realistic interactions between objects in your game world. This is crucial for implementing features like character movement, collisions, and object dynamics.

5. Game Objects: Create and manage game objects such as characters, enemies, items, and obstacles. These objects should have properties, behaviors, and interactions that define the gameplay.

Example: Basic Game Loop

```
// Initialize Three.js components (scene, camera, renderer, etc.)

function update() {
```

```
// Update game logic (e.g., move characters, check collisions)
}
function render() {
// Render the scene
renderer.render(scene, camera);
}
function gameLoop() {
// Update game state
update();
// Render the scene
render();
// Call the game loop recursively
requestAnimationFrame(gameLoop);
}
// Start the game loop
gameLoop();
```

6. User Interface: Create a user interface (UI) for your game, including HUD elements, score displays, health bars, and menus. You can use HTML/CSS for UI components and overlay them onto the 3D scene.

7. Sound and Music: Enhance the gaming experience with audio

effects and background music. Three.js allows you to integrate audio seamlessly into your games.

8. Game Design: Plan and design your game's mechanics, levels, challenges, and objectives. Balancing difficulty and ensuring a satisfying progression are key aspects of game design.

9. Testing and Debugging: Rigorous testing and debugging are crucial in game development. Use browser developer tools, debugging libraries, and playtesting to identify and fix issues.

10. Performance Optimization: Optimize your game for performance by considering factors like rendering efficiency, memory management, and minimizing computational load.

Conclusion

Incorporating game mechanics into your Three.js projects opens up exciting possibilities for creating interactive and entertaining 3D games. Whether you're building a simple arcade game or a complex simulation, understanding the principles of game development and leveraging Three.js features can help you create engaging and immersive gaming experiences. Keep in mind that game development often involves iterative design and testing to fine-tune gameplay and provide players with an enjoyable gaming experience.

Chapter 7: Working with Audio and Video

7.1 Adding Sound Effects and Music

In this section, we'll explore the integration of audio into your Three.js projects. Audio is a powerful tool for enhancing user experiences in 3D environments, whether you want to add background music, sound effects, or interactive audio elements. Three.js provides features for working with audio, making it possible to create immersive audio-visual experiences.

The Role of Audio in 3D Environments

Audio plays a vital role in creating realistic and engaging 3D environments. It adds depth and immersion by providing auditory cues that complement the visual elements. Here are some key ways in which audio contributes to the overall experience:

- **Ambiance:** Background sounds such as nature sounds, cityscapes, or music can set the mood and atmosphere of your 3D scene.

- **Feedback:** Sound effects provide feedback to user actions, making interactions more intuitive and responsive. For example, a button click or object collision can trigger a corresponding sound effect.

- **Spatial Audio:** In 3D environments, audio can be spatially positioned, creating a sense of direction and distance. This is essential for VR and immersive experiences where audio sources move with the user's perspective.

- **Narration:** Audio narration or voiceovers can guide users through interactive experiences or provide storytelling elements in 3D presentations.

Working with Audio in Three.js

Three.js provides an AudioLoader to load audio files (e.g., MP3 or WAV) and an Audio object for managing audio playback. Here's a basic example of how to add background music to your Three.js scene:

```
// Create an AudioListener to represent the user's ears

const listener = new THREE.AudioListener();

camera.add(listener);

// Create an AudioLoader and load an audio file

const audioLoader = new THREE.AudioLoader();

let backgroundMusic;

audioLoader.load('background_music.mp3', (buffer) => {

// Create an Audio object and add the audio buffer

backgroundMusic = new THREE.Audio(listener);

backgroundMusic.setBuffer(buffer);

// Set audio properties (volume, loop, etc.)

backgroundMusic.setVolume(0.5);

backgroundMusic.setLoop(true);

// Start playing the background music
```

```
backgroundMusic.play();
});
```

In this example, we create an AudioListener attached to the camera to represent the user's ears. We then use an AudioLoader to load an audio file and create an Audio object for playback. You can adjust properties like volume, loop, and position to customize the audio experience.

Sound Effects and Interactive Audio

To add sound effects and interactive audio to your 3D environment, you can follow a similar approach. Load audio files for specific events or interactions and trigger them as needed in response to user actions or scene events.

```
// Load a sound effect
const soundEffect = new THREE.Audio(listener);
audioLoader.load('sound_effect.mp3', (buffer) => {
soundEffect.setBuffer(buffer);
});
// Trigger the sound effect when a button is clicked
buttonElement.addEventListener('click', () => {
soundEffect.play();
});
```

In this example, we load a sound effect and play it when a button is clicked. You can adapt this pattern for various interactive elements in your 3D scene.

Challenges and Best Practices

When working with audio in Three.js, consider the following challenges and best practices:

- **Performance:** Audio playback can consume resources, so optimize your audio assets and manage their lifecycle to ensure smooth performance.

- **Compatibility:** Test your audio features across different browsers and devices to ensure compatibility.

- **Audio Formats:** Provide audio files in multiple formats (e.g., MP3, OGG) to support various browsers.

- **Accessibility:** Consider accessibility by providing options for users to control audio volume or mute sounds.

- **Dynamic Audio:** Experiment with dynamic audio effects like doppler shifting and spatialization to enhance realism in your 3D world.

Conclusion

Audio is a valuable component of 3D environments, adding depth, immersion, and interactivity to your Three.js projects. Whether you're creating interactive 3D games, simulations, or educational experiences, integrating audio elements can significantly enhance the user experience. By following best practices and considering performance and accessibility, you can effectively leverage audio to create compelling audio-visual interactions in your 3D web applications.

7.2 Textures from Video Sources

In this section, we'll explore the use of video sources to create textures in Three.js. Video textures allow you to apply dynamic, moving imagery to 3D objects, opening up a wide range of possibilities for interactive and immersive experiences.

Video as a Texture

Using video as a texture involves mapping a video stream onto the surface of a 3D object. This technique is particularly useful when you want to create objects with animated surfaces, simulate real-world screens or displays, or add dynamic backgrounds to your 3D scenes.

Creating Video Textures

To use a video as a texture in Three.js, you'll need a video element and a texture object. Here's a step-by-step guide on how to create a video texture:

1. **Create a Video Element:** In HTML, add a <video> element to your document. This element will host the video source.

```
<video id="video" autoplay loop>

<source src="video.mp4" type="video/mp4">

Your browser does not support the video tag.

</video>
```

In this example, we have an <video> element with the autoplay and loop attributes to ensure the video plays continuously.

1. **Create a VideoTexture:** In your JavaScript code, create a VideoTexture object by passing the <video> element as the video source.

```
// Get the video element by its ID

const video = document.getElementById('video');

// Create a VideoTexture

const videoTexture = new THREE.VideoTexture(video);
```

1. **Apply the Texture to an Object:** Now, apply the videoTexture to the material of a 3D object in your scene, such as a plane or a mesh. You can use the map property of the material to assign the video texture.

```
// Create a plane geometry

const geometry = new THREE.PlaneGeometry(5, 3);

// Create a material with the video texture

const material = new THREE.MeshBasicMaterial({ map: videoTexture });

// Create a mesh using the geometry and material

const mesh = new THREE.Mesh(geometry, material);

// Add the mesh to your scene

scene.add(mesh);
```

With these steps, you've successfully created a video texture and applied it to a 3D object. The video will play on the surface of the object, providing dynamic visuals.

Video Synchronization and Interaction

One powerful aspect of using video textures is the ability to synchronize them with user interactions or other events in your scene. For example, you can control video playback, pause, or seek to specific frames based on user actions or scripted events.

```
// Pause the video when a button is clicked

pauseButton.addEventListener('click', () => {

video.pause();

});

// Seek to a specific time in the video

seekButton.addEventListener('click', () => {

video.currentTime = 10; // Seek to 10 seconds into the video

});
```

By synchronizing video playback with your Three.js application, you can create interactive video experiences within a 3D context.

Challenges and Considerations

When working with video textures, consider the following challenges and best practices:

- **Performance:** Video playback can be resource-intensive, so optimize video file sizes and resolutions for smooth performance.

- **Browser Compatibility:** Ensure that video textures work across various web browsers and platforms.

- **Audio:** If your video has audio, consider how it should be handled in the context of your 3D scene. You may need to control audio playback separately.

- **Mobile and VR:** Be mindful of performance and compatibility on mobile devices and VR headsets, where resources may be more limited.

- **User Experience:** Design your interactions with video textures to enhance the overall user experience. Consider providing playback controls, captions, or interactive elements that respond to the video content.

Conclusion

Video textures in Three.js offer a dynamic and engaging way to bring life to your 3D scenes. Whether you're creating interactive presentations, virtual tours, or games, the ability to incorporate moving visuals can greatly enhance the user experience. By understanding how to create and control video textures, you can leverage this powerful feature to create immersive 3D web applications.

7.3 Synchronizing Audio with 3D Actions

In this section, we'll explore the synchronization of audio with 3D actions in Three.js. Synchronizing audio cues, such as sound effects or music, with specific events or interactions in your 3D scenes can greatly enhance the immersive experience. Whether you're creating interactive games, simulations, or presentations, timing audio correctly adds depth and realism to your projects.

The Role of Audio Synchronization

Audio synchronization involves playing sounds precisely at the right moment within your 3D environment. It helps create a stronger connection between the visual and auditory aspects of your application. Here are some common scenarios where audio synchronization is valuable:

- **Sound Effects:** Playing sound effects like footsteps, door openings, or explosions when specific actions occur in a game or simulation.

- **Music Transitions:** Changing background music to match the mood or context of a scene or level transition.

- **Voiceovers:** Triggering voiceovers or narrations that correspond to specific actions or events.

- **Feedback:** Providing auditory feedback to user interactions, such as button clicks or successful actions.

Basic Audio Synchronization

To synchronize audio with 3D actions in Three.js, you can use JavaScript event handlers, timers, or custom logic. Here's a basic example of how to play a sound effect when a button is clicked:

```
// Get a reference to a button element

const button = document.getElementById('myButton');
```

```
// Create an Audio object and load a sound effect
const audio = new Audio('sound-effect.mp3');
// Add a click event listener to the button
button.addEventListener('click', () => {
// Play the sound effect when the button is clicked
audio.play();
});
```

In this example, we create an Audio object, load a sound effect, and play it when the button is clicked. This approach is suitable for simple synchronization tasks but may not provide precise timing for complex interactions.

Precise Timing and Animation

For more advanced synchronization, you can leverage the animation capabilities of Three.js. By using the animation loop, you can precisely control when audio is triggered based on the progression of your animations or 3D object movements.

Here's an example of how to synchronize audio with an object's animation:

```
// Create an Audio object and load a sound effect
const audio = new Audio('sound-effect.mp3');
// Define an animation loop
function animate() {
// Update your 3D scene and objects here
```

```
// Check a condition (e.g., when an object reaches a specific position)

if (object.position.x >= 10) {

// Play the sound effect

audio.play();

}

// Continue the animation loop

requestAnimationFrame(animate);

}

// Start the animation loop

animate();
```

In this example, the sound effect is played when a specific condition is met during the animation loop. This allows you to synchronize audio precisely with the movement or actions of objects in your 3D scene.

Challenges and Considerations

When synchronizing audio with 3D actions, keep the following challenges and considerations in mind:

- **Timing Precision:** Ensure that audio cues are timed precisely to match visual events for a seamless user experience.

- **Performance:** Handling audio synchronization and playback may impact performance, so optimize audio assets and consider resource constraints.

- **Browser Compatibility:** Test audio synchronization across different browsers and platforms to ensure consistent behavior.

- **Spatial Audio:** If you're using spatial audio in VR or AR environments, ensure that audio sources move and adjust directionally with 3D objects.

- **User Experience:** Design audio interactions with user experience in mind, providing feedback that enhances immersion without overwhelming users.

Conclusion

Synchronizing audio with 3D actions in Three.js can greatly enhance the realism and engagement of your 3D web applications. Whether you're developing games, interactive simulations, or immersive experiences, precise audio timing adds depth and immersion to the user experience. By understanding the principles of audio synchronization and leveraging Three.js capabilities, you can create compelling audio-visual interactions in your 3D projects.

7.4 Interactive Audio-Visual Experiences

In this section, we'll explore the creation of interactive audio-visual experiences in Three.js. Combining both audio and visual elements in a synchronized manner can result in captivating and immersive 3D web applications. Whether you're developing interactive storytelling, educational content, or games, the synergy between audio and visuals can greatly enhance user engagement.

The Power of Interaction

Interactive audio-visual experiences are all about user engagement and participation. They allow users to influence the content they're interacting with, making the experience more personalized and engaging. Here are some ways interaction can be achieved:

- **User Input:** Actions such as mouse clicks, keyboard inputs, or touch gestures can trigger audio-visual responses.

- **Proximity and Collision:** Interactions can occur when 3D objects collide, come close to each other, or are manipulated by the user.

- **Environmental Changes:** User actions or changes in the 3D environment can lead to dynamic alterations in audio and visuals.

Creating Interactive Scenes

To build interactive audio-visual experiences in Three.js, you'll need to consider several key components:

1. **User Interface:** Design a user interface (UI) that provides control and feedback to users. UI elements can trigger audio and visual effects when interacted with.
2. **Event Handling:** Implement event listeners to capture user interactions, such as mouse clicks or keyboard inputs.
3. **Audio Synchronization:** Ensure that audio cues are synchronized with visual events. This involves precise timing and coordination between audio and visual elements.
4. **Visual Feedback:** Use animations, particle effects, shaders,

and other visual techniques to provide feedback to users.

5. **User Guidance:** Provide cues or hints to guide users on how to interact with your 3D scene and trigger audio-visual responses.

Example: Interactive Storytelling

Let's consider an example of an interactive storytelling experience in Three.js. You have a 3D scene with characters, objects, and a narrative. When the user clicks on a character, it triggers a corresponding dialogue audio and a visual animation of the character speaking. Here's a simplified implementation:

```
// Create a clickable character mesh

const character = createCharacterMesh();

scene.add(character);

// Add a click event listener

character.addEventListener('click', () => {

// Play dialogue audio

const dialogueAudio = new Audio('character_dialogue.mp3');

dialogueAudio.play();

// Trigger character animation (e.g., speaking animation)

character.playAnimation('speak');

});
```

In this example, clicking on the character triggers both audio and visual responses, enhancing the storytelling experience.

Challenges and Best Practices

When creating interactive audio-visual experiences, consider the following challenges and best practices:

- **User Guidance:** Ensure that users understand how to interact with your 3D scene. Use visual cues, tooltips, or tutorials to guide them.

- **Performance:** Balance the richness of audio-visual effects with performance optimization to ensure smooth experiences on various devices.

- **Accessibility:** Make your interactive content accessible by providing alternatives for users with disabilities, such as captions or alternative control methods.

- **Testing and Feedback:** Conduct usability testing to gather feedback from users and refine the interactive elements for a better user experience.

Conclusion

Interactive audio-visual experiences in Three.js offer a powerful way to engage users and immerse them in 3D web applications. By carefully designing interactions, synchronizing audio and visuals, and providing guidance to users, you can create compelling and memorable interactive content. Whether you're developing games, educational applications, or interactive presentations, the combination of audio and visuals can elevate the overall user experience.

7.5 Challenges and Best Practices in Audio-Visual Integration

In this section, we'll explore the challenges and best practices when integrating audio and visuals in Three.js projects. While combining audio and visuals can result in immersive experiences, it also presents various considerations to ensure a seamless and enjoyable user experience.

Synchronization and Timing

One of the primary challenges in audio-visual integration is achieving precise synchronization and timing. Ensuring that audio cues align perfectly with visual events can be challenging but is crucial for realism and immersion. To address this challenge:

- **Use Time-Based Animation:** Implement animations and audio playback based on time intervals rather than frame counts to ensure consistency across different devices and frame rates.

- **Preload Assets:** Preload audio and visual assets to reduce delays and ensure that they are ready for playback when needed.

- **Adjust for Latency:** Consider latency in audio playback and compensate for delays, especially in real-time interactive applications.

Performance Optimization

Audio-visual integration can have performance implications, impacting the overall user experience. To maintain smooth performance:

- **Optimize Assets:** Compress audio and visual assets without compromising quality to reduce file sizes and loading times.

- **Use Efficient Code:** Write efficient code to handle audio-visual synchronization and interactions without causing performance bottlenecks.

- **Manage Resources:** Control the number of simultaneous audio and visual effects to prevent resource exhaustion, particularly on mobile and low-end devices.

Cross-Browser Compatibility

Ensuring compatibility across different web browsers and platforms is essential for reaching a broader audience. To address compatibility issues:

- **Test Extensively:** Test your Three.js application with various web browsers and devices to identify and resolve compatibility issues.

- **Browser Feature Detection:** Use feature detection techniques to check for browser support for audio and visual features, providing fallbacks or alternatives where necessary.

Accessibility

Making your audio-visual content accessible to all users is a crucial consideration:

- **Captioning:** If your application includes spoken dialogue, provide captioning or subtitles for users who are deaf or hard of hearing.

- **Alternative Controls:** Consider alternative methods for controlling audio-visual interactions, such as keyboard shortcuts or touch gestures, for users with disabilities.

User Experience and Feedback

Designing for an excellent user experience is essential in audio-visual integration:

- **Usability Testing:** Conduct usability testing with users to gather feedback and identify areas for improvement in the integration of audio and visuals.

- **User Guidance:** Provide clear and intuitive user guidance to help users understand how to interact with your 3D environment and trigger audio-visual responses.

- **User Preferences:** Allow users to control audio settings, such as volume levels, muting, and audio description preferences, to personalize their experience.

Environmental Considerations

In virtual reality (VR) and augmented reality (AR) applications, environmental factors play a significant role in audio-visual integration:

- **Spatial Audio:** Implement spatial audio techniques to ensure that sound sources appear to come from the correct spatial locations in 3D space, enhancing the sense of immersion.

- **Lighting and Shading:** Consider how lighting conditions in the real world can affect the visibility and perception of visuals in AR applications.

- **Hardware Limitations:** Be aware of the limitations of VR and AR hardware, such as headset capabilities and processing power, and optimize your audio-visual content accordingly.

Conclusion

Integrating audio and visuals in Three.js projects offers the potential for creating engaging and immersive 3D web applications. However, it comes with its challenges, ranging from synchronization and performance optimization to compatibility and accessibility considerations. By adhering to best practices and addressing these challenges, you can create audio-visual experiences that captivate and delight users while delivering a seamless and inclusive experience across various platforms and devices.

Chapter 8: Physics in Three.js

8.1 Understanding Physics Engines

In this section, we'll delve into the world of physics engines and their role in Three.js development. Physics engines are essential for simulating realistic movement, collisions, and interactions in 3D environments. Whether you're creating games, simulations, or interactive experiences, understanding how physics engines work in Three.js is crucial.

The Role of Physics Engines

Physics engines are software libraries that simulate physical behaviors in a virtual environment. They apply principles of physics, such as gravity, forces, and collision detection, to objects within a 3D scene. The primary functions of a physics engine in Three.js include:

- **Collision Detection:** Identifying when objects intersect or collide with each other and responding accordingly.

- **Simulation of Forces:** Calculating and applying forces, such as gravity or user input, to objects to determine their movement.

- **Realistic Movement:** Simulating realistic movement and physics-based interactions, including rigid body dynamics, soft body physics, and constraints.

- **Energy Conservation:** Ensuring that energy is conserved in the simulation, allowing objects to react to forces and collisions realistically.

Physics Engines in Three.js

Three.js provides integration with various physics engines, making it easier to incorporate physics simulations into your 3D projects. Some of the popular physics engines supported by Three.js include Ammo.js, Cannon.js, and Oimo.js. Each engine has its features and performance characteristics, allowing you to choose the one that best suits your project's requirements.

Integrating a Physics Engine

To integrate a physics engine into your Three.js project, you typically need to follow these steps:

1. **Select a Physics Engine:** Choose a physics engine that aligns with your project's needs and familiarity.
2. **Import the Physics Engine:** Include the physics engine library in your project. This usually involves linking to a JavaScript file or installing it as a package using a package manager like npm.
3. **Create Physics Objects:** Define physics objects such as rigid bodies, constraints, and collision shapes that represent elements in your 3D scene.
4. **Initialize the Physics World:** Set up the physics world, which manages all the physics calculations, and configure its parameters such as gravity and time step.
5. **Update Physics:** In your animation loop, update the physics world by calling its step function, which advances the simulation based on the elapsed time.

```
// Example of initializing a physics world with Ammo.js

const physicsWorld = new Ammo.btDiscreteDynamicsWorld(
```

```
new Ammo.btCollisionDispatcher(),
new Ammo.btDbvtBroadphase(),
new Ammo.btSequentialImpulseConstraintSolver(),
new Ammo.btDefaultCollisionConfiguration()
);
physicsWorld.setGravity(new Ammo.btVector3(0, -9.81, 0)); // Set gravity
// Inside your animation loop
function animate() {
// Update your 3D scene
// Update the physics world
physicsWorld.stepSimulation(deltaTime, maxSubSteps);
// Continue the animation loop
requestAnimationFrame(animate);
}
```

1. **Apply Forces and Constraints:** Use the physics engine's API to apply forces, constraints, and collision callbacks as needed to achieve the desired behavior.

Physics Engine Considerations

When working with physics engines in Three.js, consider the following:

- **Performance:** Physics simulations can be computationally expensive. Optimize your scene and use appropriate collision shapes to maintain good performance.

- **Integration:** Ensure that the physics engine integrates well with your existing Three.js code and other libraries or frameworks you might be using.

- **Debugging:** Physics simulations can be challenging to debug. Most physics engines offer debugging tools to help visualize collision shapes and forces.

- **Documentation:** Familiarize yourself with the documentation and examples provided by the chosen physics engine to effectively implement physics in your Three.js project.

Conclusion

Understanding physics engines and how to integrate them into Three.js is a valuable skill for creating realistic and interactive 3D experiences. Whether you're building games, simulations, or any application that requires physics-based interactions, leveraging physics engines can add depth and realism to your projects. By following best practices and considering performance and integration, you can effectively harness the power of physics in your Three.js applications.

8.2 Integrating a Physics Engine with Three.js

In this section, we will explore the process of integrating a physics engine with Three.js to enable realistic physics simulations in your 3D web applications. Physics engines play a crucial role in handling collision detection, object interactions, and the simulation of physical forces in the virtual world.

Choosing a Physics Engine

Before integrating a physics engine into your Three.js project, you must choose the one that best suits your needs. Three.js supports various physics engines, including Ammo.js, Cannon.js, and Oimo.js. Each engine has its features, performance characteristics, and API, so your choice should align with your project's requirements and your familiarity with the engine.

Integrating Ammo.js as an Example

As an example, let's explore the integration of Ammo.js, a popular physics engine, with Three.js. Ammo.js is known for its performance and compatibility with Three.js.

Step 1: Importing Ammo.js

First, you need to include Ammo.js in your project. You can do this by including the Ammo.js library in your HTML file:

```
<script src="path/to/ammo.js"></script>
```

Step 2: Initializing the Physics World

Next, you need to create and initialize the physics world. This is where all the physics simulations will take place. You'll also configure parameters like gravity and time step.

```
// Create a physics world
```

```
const collisionConfiguration = new Ammo.btDefaultCollisionConfiguration();

const dispatcher = new Ammo.btCollisionDispatcher(collisionConfiguration);

const overlappingPairCache = new Ammo.btDbvtBroadphase();

const solver = new Ammo.btSequentialImpulseConstraintSolver();

const physicsWorld = new Ammo.btDiscreteDynamicsWorld(dispatcher, overlappingPairCache, solver, collisionConfiguration);

physicsWorld.setGravity(new Ammo.btVector3(0, -9.81, 0)); // Set gravity
```

Step 3: Creating Physics Objects

You can define physics objects like rigid bodies, constraints, and collision shapes. These objects represent elements in your 3D scene and interact with each other.

```
// Create a rigid body for a dynamic object

const mass = 1;

const startTransform = new Ammo.btTransform();

startTransform.setIdentity();

const shape = new Ammo.btSphereShape(1); // Create a sphere shape

const localInertia = new Ammo.btVector3(0, 0, 0);

shape.calculateLocalInertia(mass, localInertia);
```

const motionState = **new** Ammo.btDefaultMotionState(startTransform);

const rbInfo = **new** Ammo.btRigidBodyConstructionInfo(mass, motionState, shape, localInertia);

const rigidBody = **new** Ammo.btRigidBody(rbInfo);

// Add the rigid body to the physics world

physicsWorld.addRigidBody(rigidBody);

Step 4: Updating the Physics World

In your animation loop, you should update the physics world using the stepSimulation function to progress the physics simulation based on the elapsed time.

function animate() {

// Update your 3D scene and objects here

// Update the physics world

const deltaTime = clock.getDelta(); *// Get time elapsed since the last frame*

const maxSubSteps = 1;

const fixedTimeStep = 1 / 60; *// 60 FPS*

physicsWorld.stepSimulation(deltaTime, maxSubSteps, fixedTimeStep);

// Continue the animation loop

requestAnimationFrame(animate);

}

Step 5: Applying Forces and Constraints

You can apply forces, constraints, and collision callbacks as needed to achieve the desired behavior in your physics simulations. This may involve handling user input or scripted interactions.

```
// Apply a force to the rigid body (e.g., to simulate a jump)

const force = new Ammo.btVector3(0, 10, 0); // Upward force

rigidBody.applyCentralImpulse(force);
```

Conclusion

Integrating a physics engine like Ammo.js with Three.js allows you to create realistic and interactive 3D environments. By following the steps outlined above, you can incorporate physics simulations into your web applications, making them more engaging and dynamic. Be sure to explore the documentation and examples provided by the chosen physics engine to gain a deeper understanding of its capabilities and use cases.

8.3 Simulating Realistic Movement and Collisions

In this section, we'll dive into the details of simulating realistic movement and collisions using a physics engine in Three.js. Realistic movement and collision handling are essential for creating immersive and interactive 3D experiences, such as games and simulations.

Rigid Body Dynamics

Physics engines like Ammo.js, Cannon.js, and Oimo.js support rigid body dynamics, which simulate the movement of solid objects in response to forces and constraints. These dynamics are particularly useful for simulating objects like vehicles, characters, and rigid props.

Creating Rigid Bodies

To simulate the movement of an object, you first create a rigid body and define its properties. These properties include mass, shape, initial position, and initial velocity.

// Create a rigid body for a dynamic object

const mass = 1; *// Mass of the object*

const startTransform = **new** Ammo.btTransform(); *// Initial transform*

startTransform.setIdentity();

const shape = **new** Ammo.btBoxShape(**new** Ammo.btVector3(1, 1, 1)); *// Create a box shape*

const localInertia = **new** Ammo.btVector3(0, 0, 0);

shape.calculateLocalInertia(mass, localInertia);

const motionState = **new** Ammo.btDefaultMotionState(startTransform);

const rbInfo = **new** Ammo.btRigidBodyConstructionInfo(mass, motionState, shape, localInertia);

const rigidBody = **new** Ammo.btRigidBody(rbInfo);

```
// Add the rigid body to the physics world

physicsWorld.addRigidBody(rigidBody);
```

Applying Forces and Impulses

You can apply forces or impulses to rigid bodies to simulate interactions like pushing, pulling, or jumping. Forces are applied continuously over time, while impulses are instantaneous changes in momentum.

```
// Apply a force to the rigid body (e.g., to simulate a continuous push)

const force = new Ammo.btVector3(10, 0, 0); // Force in the x-direction

rigidBody.applyCentralForce(force);

// Apply an impulse (e.g., to simulate a jump)

const impulse = new Ammo.btVector3(0, 10, 0); // Upward impulse

rigidBody.applyCentralImpulse(impulse);
```

Collision Detection and Response

Physics engines handle collision detection and response automatically. When two objects with collision shapes intersect, the engine detects the collision and computes the appropriate response, including calculating contact points, forces, and friction.

Collision Shapes

Each rigid body in your scene should have an associated collision shape that defines its geometry for collision detection. Common collision shapes include boxes, spheres, capsules, and convex hulls.

```
// Create a collision shape for a box

const boxShape = new Ammo.btBoxShape(new Ammo.btVector3(1, 1, 1));

// Associate the collision shape with a rigid body

const rbInfo = new Ammo.btRigidBodyConstructionInfo(mass, motionState, boxShape, localInertia);

const rigidBody = new Ammo.btRigidBody(rbInfo);
```

Collision Callbacks

You can set up collision callbacks to perform custom actions when collisions occur. For example, you might play a sound effect, trigger a visual effect, or apply additional forces based on the collision.

```
// Set up a collision callback for a rigid body

rigidBody.addEventListener('collide', (event) => {

const otherObject = event.target; // The other object involved in the collision

// Perform custom actions based on the collision

playCollisionSound();

applyCollisionForce(otherObject);
```

});

Constraints and Joints

Constraints and joints allow you to simulate connections between objects, such as hinges, sliders, and ropes. These components enable you to create complex mechanical systems and interactive objects.

Creating Constraints

Constraints are defined by specifying two rigid bodies and their relative positions or axes. Common constraints include hinge constraints, slider constraints, and point-to-point constraints.

```
// Create a hinge constraint between two rigid bodies

const pivotA = new Ammo.btVector3(0, 0, 0); // Pivot point on body A

const pivotB = new Ammo.btVector3(0, 0, 0); // Pivot point on body B

const axis = new Ammo.btVector3(0, 1, 0); // Axis of rotation

const hingeConstraint = new Ammo.btHingeConstraint(bodyA, bodyB, pivotA, pivotB, axis);
```

Conclusion

Simulating realistic movement and collisions in Three.js with the help of a physics engine opens up possibilities for creating dynamic and interactive 3D environments. Understanding rigid body dynamics, collision detection, and constraints is essential for developers aiming to build engaging games, simulations, or any application that requires accurate physics simulations. By applying forces, handling collisions, and creating constraints, you can bring realism and interactivity to your Three.js projects.

8.4 Particle Systems and Effects

In this section, we'll explore particle systems and effects in Three.js, which allow you to create a wide range of visual effects, from smoke and fire to rain and explosions. Particle systems are a powerful tool for adding realism and dynamism to your 3D scenes.

What Are Particle Systems?

Particle systems simulate the behavior of individual particles, which can represent a variety of visual elements, such as dust, sparks, or raindrops. These particles are generated, updated, and rendered as a group, creating dynamic effects. Particle systems are widely used in games, simulations, and animations to simulate natural phenomena and add visual richness to scenes.

Creating a Particle System

To create a particle system in Three.js, you need to follow these general steps:

1. **Define Particle Properties:** Specify the appearance and behavior of the particles, including attributes like position, velocity, color, size, and lifetime.
2. **Generate Particles:** Create a set of particles based on the defined properties. You can generate particles at specific positions, such as the location of an explosion or the emitter of a fire effect.
3. **Update Particles:** In each frame of your animation loop, update the state of the particles according to their properties and the desired behavior. This includes updating

positions, velocities, colors, and checking for particle death.

4. **Render Particles:** Render the particles as points, sprites, or other visual representations. Apply textures and materials to make the particles look like smoke, sparks, or any desired effect.

Example: Smoke Effect

Let's consider an example of creating a simple smoke effect using a particle system in Three.js:

```
// Define particle properties

const particleCount = 1000;

const particles = new THREE.Geometry();

const particleMaterial = new THREE.PointsMaterial({

color: 0x888888,

size: 0.2,

map: new THREE.TextureLoader().load('smoke.png'), // Smoke texture

blending: THREE.AdditiveBlending,

transparent: true,

});

// Generate particles

for (let i = 0; i < particleCount; i++) {

const particle = new THREE.Vector3(
```

```
Math.random() * 5 - 2.5, // Random x position within a range

Math.random() * 5 - 2.5, // Random y position within a range

Math.random() * 5 - 2.5 // Random z position within a range

);

particle.velocity = new THREE.Vector3(0, Math.random() * 0.5, 0); // Initial upward velocity

particle.lifetime = Math.random() * 5 + 2; // Random lifetime between 2 and 7 seconds

particles.vertices.push(particle);

}

// Create the particle system

const smoke = new THREE.Points(particles, particleMaterial);

scene.add(smoke);

// Update and render the particles in your animation loop

function animate() {

// Update particle positions based on velocity

particles.vertices.forEach((particle) => {

if (particle.lifetime > 0) {

particle.add(particle.velocity);

particle.lifetime -= 0.02; // Reduce the particle's lifetime

}
```

```
});

// Render the particles

smoke.geometry.verticesNeedUpdate = true;

renderer.render(scene, camera);

// Continue the animation loop

requestAnimationFrame(animate);

}
```

Advanced Effects

Particle systems can be used to create more complex effects by adjusting parameters and behaviors. For example, by modifying particle lifetimes, colors, and sizes over time, you can create effects like fireworks or magical spells. Additionally, by applying forces, such as wind or gravity, you can simulate the behavior of particles in different environments.

Performance Considerations

While particle systems are a great tool for enhancing visuals, they can be computationally expensive, especially when dealing with a large number of particles. To maintain good performance:

- Limit the number of particles and optimize their rendering.

- Implement level-of-detail techniques to reduce the detail of particles in the distance.

- Use particle pooling to reuse particles instead of constantly creating and destroying them.

Conclusion

Particle systems and effects in Three.js offer a powerful way to add realism and dynamism to your 3D scenes. Whether you want to simulate natural phenomena like smoke and fire or create magical and fantastical effects, understanding how to create and control particle systems is essential. By defining particle properties, generating, updating, and rendering particles, you can bring your 3D environments to life and create captivating visual experiences.

8.5 Performance Optimization in Physics Simulations

In this section, we'll explore performance optimization techniques for physics simulations in Three.js. Physics simulations can be computationally expensive, especially when dealing with complex scenes or a large number of objects. Optimizing your physics simulations is crucial to maintain a smooth and responsive user experience.

1. Reduce the Number of Simulated Objects

One of the most effective ways to improve performance is to reduce the number of objects that require physics simulations. You can do this by:

- **Culling:** Implement frustum and occlusion culling techniques to skip simulating objects that are not currently visible to the camera.

- **Level of Detail (LOD):** Use LOD techniques to decrease the detail of objects that are far from the camera. Objects in the distance may not require as precise physics simulations.

2. Use Simple Collision Shapes

Choose simple collision shapes whenever possible. Complex collision shapes, such as concave meshes, can significantly impact performance. Use primitive shapes like spheres, boxes, or capsules for collision detection instead.

```
// Example of creating a simple collision shape

const collisionShape = new Ammo.btBoxShape(new Ammo.btVector3(1, 1, 1));
```

3. Limit Physics Updates

Reduce the frequency of physics updates by setting a fixed time step and updating the physics world at a consistent rate. This can help maintain stability and predictability in your simulations while optimizing performance.

```
// Example of setting a fixed time step

const fixedTimeStep = 1 / 60; // 60 FPS

physicsWorld.stepSimulation(deltaTime, maxSubSteps, fixedTimeStep);
```

4. Use Constraints Wisely

Constraints, such as hinges and sliders, add complexity to your simulations. Use them only when necessary, and consider alternatives for simple interactions. Overusing constraints can lead to decreased performance.

5. Implement Broadphase Optimization

Broadphase collision detection is the process of quickly identifying potential collisions between objects before detailed collision checks. Implement efficient broadphase algorithms, like sweep and prune or dynamic AABB trees, to reduce the number of detailed collision checks.

6. Optimize Collision Filtering

In many cases, not all objects need to collide with each other. Implement collision filtering to specify which objects should interact and which should be ignored, reducing unnecessary collision checks.

```
// Example of collision filtering

const collisionFilterGroup = 1;

const collisionFilterMask = 2;

rigidBody.setCollisionFlags(collisionFilterGroup);

rigidBody.setCollisionMask(collisionFilterMask);
```

7. Use Object Pooling

Instead of constantly creating and destroying physics objects, consider using object pooling to reuse them. Object pooling reduces memory allocation overhead and can improve performance.

8. Profile and Diagnose

Use profiling tools to identify performance bottlenecks in your physics simulations. Tools like Chrome DevTools or dedicated profiling libraries can help you pinpoint areas that require optimization.

9. Optimize Render Loops

Ensure that your rendering and physics update loops are well-optimized. Reducing the overhead in your rendering code can indirectly improve physics performance by allowing more time for physics calculations.

10. Experiment and Test

Optimization is often an iterative process. Experiment with different optimization techniques, measure their impact on performance, and test your simulations on target devices to ensure a smooth user experience.

Conclusion

Performance optimization is a crucial aspect of physics simulations in Three.js, especially when dealing with complex 3D scenes. By following these optimization techniques, you can maintain a high level of realism in your simulations while ensuring that they run smoothly on a wide range of devices. Balancing performance and visual fidelity is key to delivering engaging and responsive 3D web applications.

9.1 Understanding Real-Time vs. Pre-Rendered Graphics

In this section, we will delve into the concepts of real-time and pre-rendered graphics in the context of 3D web development. Understanding the differences between these approaches is essential for making informed decisions when creating 3D content for the web.

Real-Time Graphics

Real-time graphics, as the name suggests, involve rendering images or animations on the fly as they are needed. In the context of 3D web development, real-time graphics are generated in real-time by the user's device, typically through the use of graphics hardware and rendering APIs like WebGL.

Key Characteristics of Real-Time Graphics:

1. **Interactivity:** Real-time graphics allow for user interaction and dynamic changes in the content. Users can navigate 3D scenes, manipulate objects, and experience animations in response to their actions.
2. **Performance Requirements:** Achieving real-time rendering often requires optimizing rendering pipelines, shaders, and assets to ensure smooth and responsive experiences. This is crucial for applications like 3D games and simulations.
3. **Dynamic Lighting and Shadows:** Real-time graphics can simulate dynamic lighting and shadows, enhancing the realism of scenes. This is achieved through techniques like shadow mapping and real-time ray tracing.
4. **Procedural Content:** Real-time graphics can generate

content procedurally, allowing for the creation of vast and diverse virtual worlds without the need to pre-render every detail.

5. **Real-Time Physics:** Physics simulations can be integrated into real-time graphics to simulate realistic object behavior, collisions, and interactions.

Pre-Rendered Graphics

Pre-rendered graphics, on the other hand, involve creating and rendering 3D content in advance, often offline or during content creation. These pre-rendered images or animations are then delivered to users without further rendering on their devices.

Key Characteristics of Pre-Rendered Graphics:

1. **Offline Rendering:** Pre-rendered graphics are generated offline, using powerful hardware and rendering farms, to produce high-quality visuals that may not be achievable in real-time.
2. **Fixed Visuals:** Once pre-rendered, the visuals are fixed and do not change in response to user interactions. They are suitable for applications where user interactivity is limited.
3. **Cinematic Quality:** Pre-rendered graphics are often associated with cinematic quality, as they can incorporate complex lighting, global illumination, and high-quality textures.
4. **Non-Interactive:** Pre-rendered content is not interactive by nature. It is commonly used in applications like animated movies, architectural visualizations, and pre-rendered 360-degree videos.
5. **Large File Sizes:** High-quality pre-rendered content can

result in large file sizes, which may require efficient streaming or downloading mechanisms for web delivery.

Choosing Between Real-Time and Pre-Rendered Graphics

The choice between real-time and pre-rendered graphics depends on the goals and requirements of your 3D web project:

- If interactivity, user engagement, and dynamic content are essential, real-time graphics are the way to go. Examples include 3D games, interactive product configurators, and virtual tours.

- For cinematic-quality visuals, such as architectural visualizations, product presentations, and promotional content, pre-rendered graphics may be more suitable, as they can achieve high fidelity and realism.

- In some cases, a combination of both approaches can be used, such as integrating pre-rendered background environments with real-time interactive elements.

Understanding the strengths and limitations of each approach is crucial for making informed design and development decisions when creating 3D web experiences.

9.2 Shader Programming Basics

Shader programming is a fundamental concept in 3D graphics, and it plays a crucial role in real-time rendering using WebGL and Three.js. Shaders are small programs that run on the GPU (Graphics Processing Unit) and are responsible for the visual appearance of 3D objects and scenes. In this section, we'll explore the basics of shader programming and how it contributes to the rendering process.

What Are Shaders?

Shaders are specialized programs that perform various tasks related to rendering and visual effects. In the context of 3D graphics, two primary types of shaders are used:

1. **Vertex Shaders:** These shaders are responsible for processing each vertex (or point) in a 3D model. They can manipulate the position of vertices, compute lighting calculations, and pass data to fragment shaders.
2. **Fragment Shaders (Pixel Shaders):** Fragment shaders operate at a finer level, affecting individual pixels of the rendered image. They are responsible for determining the final color of each pixel based on lighting, textures, and other factors.

Shader Languages

Shaders are typically written in specialized languages like GLSL (OpenGL Shading Language). GLSL is a C-like language designed for high-performance GPU programming. Here's a simple example of a vertex shader and a fragment shader in GLSL:

Vertex Shader:

```
// Vertex shader

attribute vec3 position;

attribute vec3 normal;

varying vec3 vNormal;
```

```
uniform mat4 modelViewMatrix;

uniform mat4 projectionMatrix;

void main() {

vNormal = normal;

gl_Position = projectionMatrix * modelViewMatrix * vec4(position, 1.0);

}
```

Fragment Shader:

```
// Fragment shader

varying vec3 vNormal;

uniform vec3 lightDirection;

void main() {

vec3 normal = normalize(vNormal);

vec3 lightDir = normalize(lightDirection);

float intensity = dot(normal, lightDir);

gl_FragColor = vec4(intensity, intensity, intensity, 1.0);

}
```

How Shaders Work

Shaders are executed in parallel on the GPU for every vertex and pixel in a 3D scene. Here's a simplified overview of how shaders work in the rendering pipeline:

1. **Vertex Shader:** For each vertex in a 3D model, the vertex shader is called. It transforms the vertex's position from 3D space to 2D screen space and performs other calculations like lighting calculations. The output is passed to the fragment shader.
2. **Rasterization:** The GPU interpolates the values calculated by the vertex shader across the pixels of the polygons, creating fragments for each pixel.
3. **Fragment Shader:** For each fragment, the fragment shader is executed. It calculates the final color of the pixel, incorporating lighting, texture mapping, and any other effects. The result is the color of the pixel.
4. **Framebuffer:** The final pixel colors are written to the framebuffer, which is then displayed on the screen.

Shader Flexibility and Power

Shaders provide an incredible level of flexibility and control over the rendering process. With shaders, you can implement complex visual effects, simulate materials, create realistic lighting, and achieve unique artistic styles. This flexibility is what makes shaders an essential part of modern 3D graphics programming.

Integrating Shaders in Three.js

In Three.js, you can use shaders by creating ShaderMaterial objects and attaching them to your 3D objects. This allows you to customize the rendering process and achieve specific visual effects. Three.js provides a convenient way to work with shaders while abstracting many of the low-level details.

Understanding shader programming is key to advanced 3D web development, as it enables you to create visually stunning and interactive experiences. Whether you're interested in realistic lighting, special effects, or artistic expression, shaders are a powerful tool in your toolkit.

9.3 Post-Processing Effects

Post-processing effects are a crucial aspect of 3D graphics rendering in modern web applications. These effects are applied to the final rendered image to enhance visual quality, create artistic styles, or simulate real-world phenomena. In this section, we'll explore the concept of post-processing effects in Three.js and how they can be used to elevate the visual appeal of your 3D scenes.

What Are Post-Processing Effects?

Post-processing effects are a set of techniques that manipulate the rendered image after it has been generated but before it is displayed on the screen. These effects can simulate various real-world phenomena, alter colors and contrast, add blurs and glows, and create artistic filters. Post-processing is commonly used in games, simulations, and visualizations to achieve specific visual styles and enhance realism.

Key Post-Processing Techniques

1. Bloom Effect

The bloom effect simulates the scattering of light in a camera lens, resulting in a soft and radiant glow around bright objects. It's often used to create a dreamy or magical atmosphere in scenes.

2. Depth of Field

Depth of field mimics the focus effect of a camera, where objects at different distances from the camera are either sharp or blurred. This effect can add a cinematic quality to your 3D scenes by highlighting specific objects.

3. Motion Blur

Motion blur simulates the blurring effect caused by the motion of objects in a scene. It adds a sense of speed and realism to animations and is commonly used in fast-paced games.

4. Color Grading

Color grading allows you to adjust the color balance, saturation, and contrast of your scene. It's a powerful tool for setting the mood and style of your 3D environment.

5. Ambient Occlusion

Ambient occlusion simulates the soft shadows that occur in corners and crevices where objects meet. It enhances the realism of scenes by adding subtle shading and depth.

Implementing Post-Processing in Three.js

In Three.js, you can implement post-processing effects using libraries like "postprocessing.js." These libraries provide a range of built-in effects and shaders that you can apply to your rendered scene.

Here's a simplified example of how to set up post-processing effects in Three.js:

```
// Create a Three.js scene, camera, and renderer as usual

// Create a render target to hold the final post-processed image

const renderTarget = new THREE.WebGLRenderTarget(window.innerWidth, window.innerHeight);

// Create a composer for managing post-processing effects

const composer = new THREE.EffectComposer(renderer, renderTarget);

// Create and add post-processing passes to the composer

const bloomPass = new THREE.BloomPass(1.2, 25, 4, 256);

const depthOfFieldPass = new THREE.DepthOfFieldPass(camera);

composer.addPass(bloomPass);

composer.addPass(depthOfFieldPass);

// In your render loop, render the scene through the composer

function render() {

composer.render();

}

// You can toggle specific post-processing effects on and off as needed

depthOfFieldPass.enabled = false; // Disable depth of field
```

Custom Post-Processing Shaders

While libraries like "postprocessing.js" offer a variety of built-in effects, you can also create custom post-processing shaders using GLSL. This allows you to implement unique and tailored effects for your 3D scenes.

```
// Create a custom shader material

const customShader = new THREE.ShaderMaterial({

uniforms: {

tDiffuse: { value: null },

uResolution: { value: new THREE.Vector2(window.innerWidth, window.innerHeight) },

},

vertexShader: `

// Vertex shader code

void main() {

// ...

}

`,

fragmentShader: `

// Fragment shader code

uniform sampler2D tDiffuse;

uniform vec2 uResolution;
```

```
void main() {
// Your custom post-processing effect
// ...
}
`,
});
// Create a custom pass and add it to the composer
const customPass = new THREE.ShaderPass(customShader);
composer.addPass(customPass);
```

Performance Considerations

Post-processing effects can be computationally intensive, especially when multiple effects are combined. It's important to optimize your code and use these effects judiciously to ensure smooth performance, especially on less powerful devices.

In conclusion, post-processing effects are a powerful tool for enhancing the visual quality and style of your 3D web applications. Whether you aim to create realistic simulations, artistic renderings, or immersive games, understanding and utilizing post-processing can elevate your 3D scenes to the next level.

9.4 Optimizing for Real-Time Performance

Optimizing real-time performance in 3D web applications is essential to ensure that your content runs smoothly and efficiently on a wide range of devices, from high-end desktops to mobile devices.

In this section, we'll explore various techniques and best practices for optimizing the performance of your Three.js-based projects.

1. Efficient Geometry

a. Geometry Simplification: Use simplified geometry models, LOD (Level of Detail) techniques, and decimation tools to reduce the polygon count of your 3D models. This significantly improves rendering performance, especially on less powerful devices.

b. Instancing: Utilize geometry instancing to render multiple instances of the same object with a single draw call. This is beneficial for rendering objects like trees, rocks, or particles efficiently.

2. Texture Optimization

a. Texture Atlases: Combine multiple textures into a single texture atlas to reduce the number of texture switches during rendering. Minimize texture resolution for objects that don't require high detail.

b. Texture Compression: Use texture compression formats (e.g., ETC, ASTC, PVRTC) to reduce memory consumption and improve rendering speed, especially on mobile devices.

3. Shader Optimization

a. Shader Minification: Minify your GLSL shaders to remove unnecessary whitespace and comments, reducing shader file sizes and improving load times.

b. Shader Batching: Combine multiple shaders into a single shader program when possible. Fewer shader switches result in better performance.

c. Shader Complexity: Keep shader complexity in check. Complex shaders with multiple texture lookups and calculations can be demanding on the GPU. Profile and optimize shaders as needed.

4. Render Loop Optimization

a. RequestAnimationFrame: Use the requestAnimationFrame method for your render loop to synchronize rendering with the browser's refresh rate, improving performance and reducing unnecessary rendering.

b. Frustum Culling: Implement frustum culling to skip rendering objects that are outside the camera's view frustum. This prevents rendering off-screen objects and boosts performance.

5. LOD and Occlusion

a. Level of Detail (LOD): Implement LOD techniques to display simplified versions of objects that are distant from the camera. This reduces the rendering workload for objects in the distance.

b. Occlusion Culling: Use occlusion culling techniques to determine which objects are occluded by others and don't need to be rendered. This can significantly improve performance in complex scenes.

6. Mobile Optimization

a. Mobile-First Design: Consider mobile devices as your target platform from the beginning of your project. Optimize textures, shaders, and geometry for mobile performance.

b. Touch Controls: Implement touch-friendly controls and gestures for mobile users to enhance the user experience on touch screens.

7. Scene Management

a. Scene Complexity: Avoid overly complex scenes with too many objects and high-resolution textures. Keep scenes well-organized and optimize assets.

b. Scene Hierarchy: Optimize the scene hierarchy and object updates. Use object pools for frequently created and destroyed objects to reduce memory allocation overhead.

8. Profiling and Diagnostics

a. Performance Profiling: Use browser developer tools and profiling tools like Chrome DevTools or WebGL debugging extensions to identify performance bottlenecks and optimize code accordingly.

b. GPU Profiling: Profile GPU performance to identify shader or rendering issues that may impact frame rates. Tools like the WebGL Inspector can help.

9. WebAssembly and Multi-Threading

a. WebAssembly: Consider using WebAssembly to offload CPU-intensive tasks to a separate thread, improving overall application responsiveness.

b. Multi-Threading: Explore the potential of multi-threading for

tasks like physics simulations or AI computations to better utilize multi-core processors.

10. Testing and User Feedback

a. Device Testing: Test your 3D web application on a variety of devices and browsers to ensure compatibility and optimal performance.

b. User Feedback: Collect user feedback to identify performance issues and address them in updates.

Optimizing for real-time performance is an ongoing process in 3D web development. By following these techniques and best practices, you can create 3D applications that deliver a smooth and responsive experience to users across different devices and platforms. Balancing performance and visual fidelity is crucial for creating engaging and accessible 3D web content.

9.5 Utilizing WebGL2 Features

WebGL2 is the second version of the WebGL API, and it introduces several new features and enhancements that can benefit your Three.js projects. In this section, we'll explore some of the WebGL2 features and how you can leverage them to enhance the performance and capabilities of your 3D web applications.

1. Multiple Render Targets (MRT)

WebGL2 allows you to render to multiple textures (color attachments) in a single pass, which can be useful for advanced rendering techniques like deferred shading and post-processing effects. In Three.js, you can create and manage multiple render targets using the WebGLRenderTarget class. This feature enables you to implement complex rendering pipelines with greater flexibility.

2. Instanced Rendering

Instanced rendering is a powerful feature in WebGL2 that allows you to render multiple instances of the same object with a single draw call. This significantly reduces CPU overhead and improves rendering performance, especially when you need to render large numbers of similar objects, such as trees or particles. Three.js provides support for instanced rendering, making it easier to take advantage of this feature.

3. Transform Feedback

WebGL2 introduces transform feedback, which enables you to capture the results of vertex processing and use them as input for subsequent rendering passes. This can be useful for creating particle systems, simulations, and other dynamic effects. Three.js provides a convenient interface for working with transform feedback in WebGL2.

4. Uniform Buffer Objects (UBOs)

Uniform Buffer Objects allow you to efficiently manage and update uniform data shared across multiple shaders. Instead of setting individual uniforms for each shader, you can group related data into UBOs and update them once, improving rendering performance and reducing CPU overhead. Three.js provides support for UBOs in WebGL2.

5. Improved Textures

WebGL2 enhances texture capabilities by supporting 3D textures, array textures, and mipmapping for all texture types. These improvements enable you to work with more complex texture data and efficiently manage texture resources in your 3D scenes.

6. WebGL2 Shading Language (GLSL 3.00)

WebGL2 introduces a new version of the GLSL shading language (GLSL ES 3.00), which provides additional features and optimizations compared to the previous version. You can take advantage of these enhancements to write more efficient and expressive shader code in Three.js.

7. Geometry Shader

While WebGL1 lacked support for geometry shaders, WebGL2 introduces this feature. Geometry shaders allow you to generate and manipulate geometry on the GPU, opening up possibilities for procedural geometry generation and advanced rendering techniques.

8. Debugging and Profiling

WebGL2 offers improved debugging and profiling tools compared to WebGL1. You can use the WebGL2 debugging extensions and browser developer tools to diagnose and optimize your 3D web applications more effectively.

9. Enhanced WebGL Context

WebGL2 provides a more capable and modern rendering context compared to WebGL1. It includes improved support for WebGL extensions, better resource management, and additional rendering features that contribute to better performance and flexibility.

10. Compatibility Considerations

While WebGL2 offers many advantages, it's important to note that not all devices and browsers support it. Before using WebGL2 features, consider fallback mechanisms or feature detection to ensure that your application remains accessible to users on WebGL1-capable devices.

In conclusion, WebGL2 brings significant enhancements to the world of 3D web development, providing improved performance and capabilities for your Three.js projects. By leveraging the features of WebGL2 and Three.js, you can create more advanced and engaging 3D web applications that take full advantage of modern web technologies.

Chapter 10: Virtual Reality and Three.js

10.1 Introduction to WebVR and WebXR

Virtual Reality (VR) and Augmented Reality (AR) have emerged as exciting technologies that offer immersive and interactive experiences. In this section, we'll dive into the world of VR and explore how Three.js can be used in combination with WebVR and WebXR to create captivating virtual reality experiences for the web.

What Is WebVR and WebXR?

WebVR and **WebXR** are APIs that enable virtual and augmented reality experiences within web browsers. WebVR was the initial standard, designed for virtual reality devices, while WebXR is the evolution of that standard, encompassing both VR and AR devices.

These APIs provide a bridge between the web browser and VR/AR hardware, allowing web developers to create VR and AR experiences that can be accessed directly through a web browser, eliminating the need for dedicated applications.

Key Concepts in VR and AR

Before diving into the technical details of WebVR and WebXR, it's essential to understand some key concepts:

1. **Virtual Reality (VR):** VR immerses users in a fully virtual environment, blocking out the physical world entirely. Users typically wear a VR headset that tracks their head movements, providing a 360-degree view of the virtual world.
2. **Augmented Reality (AR):** AR overlays digital content onto the real world, enhancing the user's perception of reality. AR experiences can be accessed through devices like smartphones or AR glasses.
3. **Headsets:** VR headsets, such as the Oculus Rift or HTC Vive, provide stereoscopic displays and positional tracking to create a realistic sense of presence. AR headsets, like Microsoft HoloLens, blend digital content with the real world.
4. **Controllers:** VR and AR controllers allow users to interact with the virtual or augmented environment. These controllers can have buttons, triggers, and motion tracking.
5. **Pose and Movement Tracking:** Accurate tracking of the user's head and body movements is crucial for creating a convincing VR or AR experience. This tracking is typically

performed by sensors in the headset and controllers.

WebVR and WebXR in Three.js

Three.js provides built-in support for WebVR and WebXR, making it relatively straightforward to create VR and AR experiences for the web. You can use the WebVRManager and WebXRManager classes to handle the rendering and interaction aspects of VR and AR in your Three.js projects.

In the case of WebVR, you can use the WebVRButton class to create a VR mode button that allows users to switch between standard and VR viewing modes.

Here's a simplified example of how to set up WebVR in Three.js:

```
// Create a Three.js scene, camera, and objects as usual

// Initialize the WebVR manager

const vrButton = new THREE.WebVRButton(renderer);

document.body.appendChild(vrButton);

// Render loop

function animate() {

if (vrButton.isPresenting()) {

// Update VR scene when in VR mode

vrControls.update();

} else {

// Update non-VR scene
```

```
}
renderer.render(scene, camera);
vrButton.requestAnimationFrame(animate);
}
animate();
```

In the case of WebXR, you can use the XRButton class in a similar way to enable XR mode in your Three.js application.

Creating Immersive VR and AR Experiences

With WebVR and WebXR support in Three.js, you can create a wide range of immersive experiences, from virtual tours and games to educational simulations and product visualizations. These technologies open up new possibilities for web developers to engage users in innovative ways, and they continue to evolve with the latest advancements in VR and AR hardware.

10.2 Setting Up a VR Scene in Three.js

Creating a virtual reality (VR) scene in Three.js involves setting up the necessary components to render a 3D environment that can be experienced through a VR headset. In this section, we'll explore the steps to create a basic VR scene using Three.js, including setting up the scene, camera, and controls for VR interaction.

1. Initialize a Three.js Scene

To get started, create a Three.js scene as you would for a standard 3D application. This involves setting up a scene, camera, and renderer. You can use the following code as a template:

```
// Create a scene
const scene = new THREE.Scene();
// Create a camera
const camera = new THREE.PerspectiveCamera(75, window.innerWidth / window.innerHeight, 0.1, 1000);
camera.position.set(0, 1.6, 3);
// Create a WebGL renderer
const renderer = new THREE.WebGLRenderer();
renderer.setSize(window.innerWidth, window.innerHeight);
document.body.appendChild(renderer.domElement);
```

2. Add 3D Objects

Next, add 3D objects to your scene. These objects can be anything you want to display in your VR environment, such as models, meshes, or geometries. Here's an example of adding a simple cube to the scene:

```
const cubeGeometry = new THREE.BoxGeometry();
const cubeMaterial = new THREE.MeshBasicMaterial({ color: 0x00ff00 });
const cube = new THREE.Mesh(cubeGeometry, cubeMaterial);
scene.add(cube);
```

3. Set Up WebVR

To enable WebVR in your Three.js project, you'll need to include the WebVR library. Add the following script tag to your HTML file to include it:

```
<script src="https://cdnjs.cloudflare.com/ajax/libs/three.js/r128/vr/WebVR.js"></script>
```

4. Enable VR Mode

To allow users to enter VR mode, create a VR button and add it to your web page. Three.js provides a convenient WebVRButton class for this purpose. Here's how to set up the VR button:

```
// Create a WebVR button

const vrButton = new THREE.WebVRButton(renderer);

document.body.appendChild(vrButton.domElement);
```

5. Implement VR Controls

To enable user interaction in your VR scene, you can use VR controllers and VR headset tracking. Three.js provides the VRControls class for handling VR headset tracking and VRController for handling controllers. Here's an example of setting up VR controls:

```
// Create VR controls for the camera

const vrControls = new THREE.VRControls(camera);

// Connect the VR controls to the VR button

vrButton.setController(vrControls);
```

6. Update the Render Loop

Lastly, update your render loop to include VR rendering when in VR mode. This involves rendering the scene for each eye and updating the VR controls. Here's how to modify your render loop:

```
function animate() {

if (vrButton.isPresenting()) {

// Render for each eye

renderer.vr.enabled = true;

renderer.setAnimationLoop(render);

} else {

// Render in non-VR mode

renderer.vr.enabled = false;

renderer.render(scene, camera);

}

}

function render() {

// Update VR controls

vrControls.update();

// Render the scene for each eye

renderer.render(scene, camera);

}
```

animate();

With these steps, you've set up a basic VR scene in Three.js that users can experience using a VR headset. You can further enhance your VR environment by adding interactive elements, more complex 3D models, and custom shaders to create immersive and engaging VR experiences on the web.

10.3 Designing for VR: Best Practices

When creating virtual reality (VR) experiences with Three.js, it's essential to consider best practices to ensure that your VR content provides users with an immersive and comfortable experience. VR is a unique medium that requires special attention to factors like user comfort, interaction design, and performance optimization. In this section, we'll explore key considerations and best practices for designing VR content in Three.js.

1. Comfort and Motion Sickness

Motion sickness is a common concern in VR. To reduce the risk of discomfort for users, consider the following:

- **Frame Rate:** Maintain a consistent and high frame rate (usually 90Hz or higher) to ensure smooth visuals. Low frame rates can contribute to motion sickness.

- **Teleportation:** Implement teleportation or other locomotion techniques that minimize artificial movement. Teleportation allows users to move in VR by selecting a location to "jump" to, reducing motion sickness associated with walking or running.

- **Field of View (FoV):** Be mindful of the user's field of view. Rapid and unnatural FoV changes can lead to discomfort. Gradual transitions are often better tolerated.

- **Acceleration and Deceleration:** Avoid abrupt acceleration and deceleration in VR experiences, as these can trigger motion sickness. Implement gradual changes in velocity.

2. User Interface (UI) and Interaction

Effective UI design and user interaction are crucial for a smooth VR experience:

- **UI Placement:** Place UI elements within the user's field of view and ensure they are readable and accessible without requiring strenuous head movements.

- **Controller Interaction:** Utilize VR controllers for intuitive interaction. Map controller actions to meaningful interactions within your VR environment.

- **Reticle or Laser Pointer:** Implement a reticle or laser pointer for accurate object selection and interaction. This aids users in pointing to and interacting with virtual objects.

- **Hand Tracking:** If supported by the VR hardware, consider implementing hand tracking for more natural and immersive interactions.

3. Performance Optimization

Optimizing performance is essential for VR content:

- **Simplify Geometry:** Use lower-poly models and simplified geometry to maintain a high frame rate. Complex geometry can be taxing on the GPU and lead to performance issues.

- **Texture Resolution:** Be mindful of texture resolution. High-resolution textures may impact performance, especially on mobile VR devices.

- **Shader Complexity:** Keep shaders efficient and avoid complex shader operations that may cause frame drops.

- **Occlusion Culling:** Implement occlusion culling to avoid rendering objects that are not within the user's view, optimizing performance.

4. Comfort Modes

Consider providing comfort settings that users can customize:

- **Field of View Options:** Allow users to adjust the FoV settings to match their comfort level.

- **Locomotion Options:** Provide different locomotion options (e.g., teleportation, smooth movement, or snap turning) that users can choose based on their comfort preferences.

5. User Testing

User testing is essential to gather feedback and iterate on your VR experience:

- **User Feedback:** Collect feedback from users to identify any discomfort or usability issues and make necessary improvements.

- **Iterative Design:** Continuously refine your VR content based on user feedback and testing results.

6. Platform Considerations

Be aware of the target platform and its capabilities:

- **Hardware Compatibility:** Ensure your VR content is compatible with the target VR hardware and platforms (e.g., Oculus Rift, HTC Vive, or Oculus Quest).

- **WebVR/WebXR Support:** If creating web-based VR content, ensure compatibility with WebVR or WebXR for seamless browser-based experiences.

By following these best practices and considering user comfort, interaction design, and performance optimization, you can create compelling and enjoyable VR experiences using Three.js. Remember that VR is a dynamic and evolving field, so staying updated with the latest developments and user preferences is key to success in VR content creation.

10.4 Interaction Models in VR

In virtual reality (VR) experiences created with Three.js, interaction models play a critical role in enhancing user engagement and immersion. Interaction models define how users can interact with the virtual environment and objects within it. In this section, we'll explore various interaction models commonly used in VR and how to implement them using Three.js.

1. Controller-Based Interaction

Controller-based interaction is one of the most common methods for user interaction in VR. It involves using handheld controllers, such as those provided with VR headsets like the Oculus Touch or HTC Vive controllers, to interact with the virtual world. Three.js provides built-in support for handling VR controllers.

Here's a basic outline of how to implement controller-based interaction in Three.js:

- Initialize VR controllers and link them to the user's hands.
- Map controller buttons and triggers to specific actions, such as grabbing, pointing, or selecting objects.
- Implement logic to respond to controller inputs. For example, when the user presses a button, you can trigger an action like picking up an object.

2. Hand Tracking

Hand tracking is a more natural and immersive form of interaction in VR. Some VR headsets, like the Oculus Quest, support hand tracking, allowing users to use their real hands to interact with the virtual world. To implement hand tracking in Three.js:

- Check if the VR hardware supports hand tracking.
- Create virtual hand models that match the user's real hand positions and movements.
- Implement gesture recognition to detect hand movements and gestures for various interactions.

3. Gaze-Based Interaction

Gaze-based interaction relies on the user's gaze (where they are looking) to trigger actions or select objects in the VR environment. This can be useful for experiences that aim to minimize the need for physical controllers. To implement gaze-based interaction:

- Implement a reticle or laser pointer that follows the user's gaze direction.
- Detect when the user's gaze intersects with interactive objects.
- Trigger actions or select objects when the gaze intersects with them.

4. Teleportation and Locomotion

Navigating in VR is essential, and teleportation is a common locomotion technique that allows users to move within the virtual environment. To implement teleportation in Three.js:

- Create a teleportation system that allows users to select a destination point.
- Teleport the user to the selected location while ensuring smooth transitions to reduce motion sickness.

5. Object Interaction

Object interaction involves allowing users to interact with virtual objects within the environment. This can include picking up objects, moving them, rotating them, or triggering actions on them. To implement object interaction:

- Implement physics-based interactions to simulate realistic object behaviors.
- Use raycasting to detect when controllers or hands intersect with objects.
- Apply forces or constraints to objects based on user interactions.

6. Menu and UI Interaction

Designing user interfaces (UI) for VR is essential, and UI elements should be interactive and easy to use. To implement UI interaction:

- Create VR-friendly UI components that are easy to read and interact with.
- Implement UI interactions that match the input method, whether it's controller-based or gaze-based.
- Ensure that UI elements are appropriately positioned within the user's field of view.

7. Haptic Feedback

Haptic feedback enhances the sense of touch and realism in VR interactions. Many VR controllers provide haptic feedback, allowing you to simulate tactile sensations when users interact with objects or the environment. To implement haptic feedback:

- Map haptic feedback to specific interactions or events.
- Adjust the intensity and duration of haptic feedback based on the context of the interaction.

By considering these interaction models and implementing them effectively in your Three.js VR experiences, you can create engaging and immersive VR content that users will find enjoyable and intuitive to interact with. Experimenting with different interaction models and gathering user feedback can help you refine and optimize your VR experiences for maximum user satisfaction.

10.5 Overcoming Challenges in VR Development

Developing virtual reality (VR) experiences using Three.js is an exciting endeavor, but it comes with its share of challenges. Overcoming these challenges is essential to create immersive and enjoyable VR content. In this section, we'll explore some common challenges in VR development and strategies to address them.

1. Performance Optimization

VR requires consistently high frame rates to avoid motion sickness and provide a smooth experience. Achieving high performance is a top priority:

- **Optimize Geometry:** Keep the polygon count low by using simplified models and meshes. Minimize unnecessary detail in 3D assets.

- **Texture Optimization:** Use efficient texture formats and sizes to reduce GPU memory usage. Consider texture atlases and compression techniques.

- **Shader Complexity:** Keep shaders simple and efficient. Avoid complex shader operations that can impact performance.

- **Occlusion Culling:** Implement occlusion culling to avoid rendering objects that are not visible to the user.

- **VR-Specific Performance Profiling:** Use VR-specific performance profiling tools to identify bottlenecks and optimize accordingly.

2. Motion Sickness Mitigation

Motion sickness can be a significant challenge in VR. To mitigate motion sickness:

- **Smooth Locomotion:** Implement smooth locomotion techniques like teleportation or gradual acceleration and deceleration.

- **Comfort Modes:** Provide comfort settings, such as field of view adjustments or teleportation options, to accommodate users with varying levels of tolerance.

- **Gaze-Based Interaction:** Use gaze-based interaction instead of controller-based navigation when appropriate to reduce motion sickness.

- **Testing and Feedback:** Conduct user testing to identify discomfort triggers and iterate on your VR experience accordingly.

3. User Interface (UI) Design

Designing effective UI for VR can be challenging due to the unique requirements of the medium:

- **VR-Friendly UI:** Create UI elements that are legible, easy to interact with, and designed for the VR environment.

- **Spatial UI:** Use spatial UI techniques to place UI elements within the user's field of view, making them accessible without excessive head movement.

- **Controller Mapping:** Map UI interactions to VR controllers in an intuitive manner. Consider user feedback and iterate on UI design.

4. Content Creation

Creating 3D content for VR can be time-consuming and complex:

- **3D Modeling Tools:** Familiarize yourself with 3D modeling tools like Blender, Maya, or 3ds Max to create custom assets.

- **Asset Optimization:** Optimize 3D models and textures for real-time rendering, taking into account performance constraints.

- **Importing External Models:** Learn how to import external 3D models into your Three.js project for added complexity and variety.

5. Cross-Platform Compatibility

Ensuring your VR content works across different VR headsets and platforms can be challenging:

- **WebVR/WebXR:** Leverage WebVR and WebXR standards to create web-based VR experiences that can run on various VR headsets.

- **Device Compatibility:** Test your VR content on different VR hardware to ensure compatibility and adjust for platform-specific differences.

- **Performance Scaling:** Implement performance scaling options for lower-end VR devices to reach a broader audience.

6. User Comfort

User comfort is paramount in VR:

- **Ergonomic Design:** Ensure that users can wear VR headsets comfortably for extended periods. Consider factors like weight distribution and adjustable straps.

- **IPD Adjustment:** Provide an option for users to adjust interpupillary distance (IPD) to match their own, enhancing visual comfort.

- **Audio Quality:** High-quality spatial audio can enhance immersion and comfort. Invest in good audio design for your VR experiences.

- **Safety Guidelines:** Include safety guidelines in your VR content to remind users to take breaks and maintain awareness of their physical surroundings.

By addressing these challenges and considering best practices, you can create VR experiences that are not only immersive and engaging but also comfortable and accessible to a wide range of users. VR development is an evolving field, so staying informed about new technologies and user preferences is crucial to successful VR content creation.

Chapter 11: Augmented Reality with Three.js

11.1 Fundamentals of Augmented Reality

Augmented Reality (AR) is an exciting technology that overlays digital information and virtual objects onto the real world. It offers a unique and interactive user experience, blending the physical and digital realms. In this section, we will delve into the fundamentals of Augmented Reality and explore how to integrate AR into web applications using Three.js.

What is Augmented Reality?

Augmented Reality is a technology that enhances the real-world environment with computer-generated information, such as 3D objects, text, images, or videos. Unlike Virtual Reality (VR), which immerses users in entirely virtual environments, AR enriches the real world by superimposing digital content onto it. This can be achieved through various devices, including smartphones, tablets, AR glasses, and more.

AR applications can range from simple informational overlays, like displaying product details when scanning a barcode, to complex interactive experiences, such as interactive gaming and architectural visualization.

AR in Web Applications

Integrating AR into web applications has become increasingly popular due to its accessibility and versatility. With Three.js, you can harness the power of AR directly in web browsers, reaching a broad audience without the need for specialized hardware or apps.

To create AR experiences on the web, you'll need to leverage device features like the camera and sensors to track and understand the real-world environment. Three.js provides tools and APIs that make this integration seamless.

Getting Started with AR in Three.js

Before diving into AR development with Three.js, you'll need to set up your development environment and ensure compatibility with AR-capable devices. This typically involves using technologies like WebXR and WebAR, which provide the necessary APIs for AR interactions.

Here's a basic outline of the steps to get started with AR in Three.js:

1. **Device Compatibility:** Check if the user's device supports AR features. You can use the navigator.xr API to detect AR capabilities.
2. **Initialization:** Initialize the AR environment using Three.js and WebXR. Set up the camera and scene to render AR content.
3. **AR Tracking:** Utilize device sensors, such as the camera, gyroscope, and accelerometer, to track the user's position and orientation in the real world. Three.js simplifies this process through its XR classes.
4. **Rendering:** Overlay 3D objects or information onto the real-world view. Three.js makes it easy to create and position virtual objects in the AR scene.
5. **Interaction:** Implement user interactions, such as tapping or dragging, to interact with AR elements. You can use Three.js event handling for this purpose.
6. **Optimization:** Optimize your AR experience for performance and responsiveness, considering factors like

frame rate and rendering quality.

AR Use Cases

Augmented Reality has a wide range of use cases across various industries. Some common examples include:

- **Retail:** Allow customers to visualize products in their real environment before making a purchase decision.
- **Education:** Create interactive educational content, such as anatomy models that students can explore in AR.
- **Gaming:** Develop location-based AR games that encourage players to explore their surroundings.
- **Architecture:** Visualize architectural designs in the context of the actual construction site.
- **Navigation:** Provide real-time directions and information overlaid on the user's view.

As you explore AR development with Three.js, consider the specific use case and audience you're targeting to create compelling and engaging AR experiences.

11.2 Integrating AR in Web Applications

Augmented Reality (AR) integration into web applications has opened up new possibilities for interactive and immersive user experiences. In this section, we will explore the practical steps involved in integrating AR into web applications using Three.js and other web technologies.

Choosing the Right Framework

When integrating AR into web applications, it's essential to choose the right framework or library that supports AR features. Three.js is a popular choice due to its capabilities for 3D rendering and interaction. Additionally, you'll often leverage WebXR and WebAR APIs to access AR functionalities.

Setting Up Your Development Environment

Before diving into AR development, ensure you have the necessary tools and environment set up. You will need:

1. **Code Editor:** Choose a code editor or integrated development environment (IDE) that you are comfortable with. Common choices include Visual Studio Code, Sublime Text, or Atom.
2. **Node.js:** Node.js is often used for server-side scripting and managing dependencies. You may need it for certain AR projects.
3. **Version Control:** Consider using a version control system like Git to track changes in your codebase.

WebXR and WebAR

WebXR is a standard that provides access to augmented and virtual reality (AR/VR) devices through the web browser. WebAR is a subset of WebXR specifically focused on Augmented Reality. These APIs enable you to access AR capabilities of devices such as smartphones, tablets, and AR glasses.

To start using WebXR and WebAR in your web application, you'll typically perform the following steps:

1. **Feature Detection:** Check if the user's device supports WebXR and WebAR features. You can use the navigator.xr object for feature detection.
2. **Session Initialization:** Initialize an XR session, which represents the AR or VR experience. Use navigator.xr.requestSession() to start an AR session.
3. **Session Configuration:** Configure the AR session by specifying options like tracking type, rendering mode, and more. This depends on your application's requirements.
4. **AR Camera Setup:** Set up the camera and scene for AR rendering. You may use Three.js to create and manipulate 3D content in the AR view.
5. **AR Tracking:** Leverage the device's sensors (camera, gyroscope, accelerometer) to track the user's position and orientation in the real world. WebXR provides APIs for this purpose.
6. **Rendering AR Content:** Overlay 3D objects, images, or information onto the real-world view. Three.js makes it easy to create and position virtual objects.
7. **User Interaction:** Implement interactions with AR content, such as tapping, dragging, or gesture recognition. You can use Three.js event handling for user input.
8. **Optimization:** Ensure that your AR experience is optimized for performance and responsiveness. Consider factors like frame rate, rendering quality, and resource usage.

Libraries and Resources

When integrating AR into your web application, you can take advantage of various libraries and resources to simplify the development process. Some helpful resources include:

- **AR.js:** A JavaScript library that enables marker-based AR experiences in the browser.

- **A-Frame:** A web framework for building VR and AR experiences using HTML and entities.

- **Three.js AR Examples:** Explore Three.js AR examples and documentation to learn more about AR development.

- **WebXR Samples:** WebXR provides official samples and demos that showcase its capabilities.

Use Cases for AR in Web Applications

AR integration can enhance various types of web applications, including:

- **E-commerce:** Let customers visualize products in their real environment before making a purchase.

- **Education:** Create interactive educational content, such as AR-based learning modules.

- **Gaming:** Develop location-based AR games that encourage exploration and interaction.

- **Navigation:** Provide real-time directions and information overlaid on the user's view.

- **Marketing:** Create engaging marketing campaigns with interactive AR elements.

The choice of use case will influence the design and development of your AR web application. Tailor your approach to meet the specific needs and expectations of your target audience.

11.3 Creating Interactive AR Content

Creating interactive Augmented Reality (AR) content is at the core of delivering engaging AR experiences to users. In this section, we'll explore the techniques and strategies for designing and developing interactive AR content using Three.js and related technologies.

Design Principles for Interactive AR

Before diving into the technical aspects of creating interactive AR content, it's crucial to consider design principles that enhance user engagement:

1. **User-Centered Design:** Start with a clear understanding of your target audience and their needs. Design AR interactions that provide value and solve specific user problems.
2. **Simplicity:** Keep interactions simple and intuitive. Avoid overwhelming users with complex gestures or interactions. Make it easy for users to understand and navigate the AR experience.
3. **Feedback:** Provide visual and auditory feedback to confirm user actions. Feedback helps users understand that their interactions are having an impact on the AR content.
4. **Realism:** Strive for realism in AR interactions. Make virtual objects behave as users would expect them to in the real world. This enhances immersion.
5. **Scalability:** Design AR content that can scale to different devices and screen sizes. Ensure that interactions work

smoothly on various platforms.

Interaction Techniques

Interactivity in AR can be achieved through various techniques and input methods:

1. **Touch and Gestures:** Utilize touch gestures like tapping, swiping, pinching, and dragging to interact with AR objects. These gestures are intuitive and work well on touchscreen devices.
2. **Voice Commands:** Implement voice recognition to allow users to control and interact with AR content using their voice. This can be especially useful in hands-free scenarios.
3. **Hand Tracking:** Some AR devices support hand tracking, allowing users to interact with virtual objects using their hand movements and gestures.
4. **Object Recognition:** Use image or object recognition to trigger AR interactions when specific objects or markers are detected by the camera.
5. **Spatial Anchors:** AR experiences can be anchored to real-world locations. Users can interact with content that is tied to specific physical places, like a museum exhibit or a city landmark.
6. **Controller Input:** In AR setups with controllers, users can interact with AR content using handheld controllers, similar to VR experiences.

Implementing Interaction in Three.js

Three.js provides a robust framework for implementing interactivity in AR experiences. Here's a simplified example of how to create an interactive AR button using Three.js and WebXR:

// Initialize AR session and Three.js scene

const session = **await** navigator.xr.requestSession('immersive-ar');

const xrReferenceSpace = **await** session.requestReferenceSpace('viewer');

const xrRenderer = **new** THREE.WebXRRenderer({ xrSession: session });

// Create a button mesh

const buttonGeometry = **new** THREE.BoxGeometry(0.1, 0.05, 0.01);

const buttonMaterial = **new** THREE.MeshBasicMaterial({ color: 0x00ff00 });

const buttonMesh = **new** THREE.Mesh(buttonGeometry, buttonMaterial);

buttonMesh.position.set(0, 0, -1); *// Position the button in AR space*

// Add the button to the scene

xrReferenceSpace.addEventListener('selectstart', () => {

// Perform an action when the button is selected (e.g., change its color)

buttonMaterial.color.set(0xff0000);

});

xrReferenceSpace.addEventListener('selectend', () => {

// Reset the button's color when the selection ends

buttonMaterial.color.set(0x00ff00);

```
});

xrRenderer.scene.add(buttonMesh);

// Start rendering the AR scene

session.requestAnimationFrame(onXRFrame);

function onXRFrame(time, frame) {

const pose = frame.getViewerPose(xrReferenceSpace);

if (pose) {

xrRenderer.render(frame, pose);

}

session.requestAnimationFrame(onXRFrame);

}
```

In this example, we initialize an AR session, create a button mesh, and add event listeners for selectstart and selectend events to make the button interactive. When the user selects the button in AR space, its color changes, providing feedback.

Testing and Iteration

Creating interactive AR content often involves a significant amount of testing and iteration. It's essential to test your AR experience on various devices and gather user feedback to improve usability and engagement. Additionally, consider accessibility considerations, ensuring that your AR interactions are inclusive and usable by all users.

By following design principles, choosing appropriate interaction techniques, and leveraging Three.js and related technologies, you can create immersive and engaging interactive AR content that captivates your audience.

11.4 AR User Experience Considerations

When developing Augmented Reality (AR) applications with Three.js, it's crucial to prioritize the user experience (UX) to ensure that users have a seamless and enjoyable interaction with your AR content. In this section, we'll explore various AR UX considerations and best practices to enhance the overall quality of your AR experiences.

Spatial Understanding

One of the key challenges in AR development is creating a sense of spatial understanding. Users should intuitively grasp the relationships between real-world objects and virtual content. Consider the following:

- **Depth Perception:** Use techniques like shadows and lighting to convey depth in the AR scene. This helps users perceive how far virtual objects are from real-world objects.

- **Object Anchoring:** Ensure that virtual objects align with and interact convincingly with real-world objects. Use spatial anchors to position AR content accurately.

- **Scaling:** Virtual objects should have appropriate scaling in relation to the real world. Overly large or small objects can disrupt the sense of immersion.

Realism and Consistency

Strive for realism in your AR experiences, but also maintain consistency to avoid breaking the illusion. Consider the following:

- **Physics Simulation:** Implement realistic physics behaviors for virtual objects. For example, objects should fall to the ground and react to collisions as expected.

- **Lighting and Shadows:** Use proper lighting and shadow rendering to make virtual objects blend seamlessly with the real world. Ensure that lighting matches the physical environment.

- **Sound Design:** Incorporate spatial audio to enhance the sense of presence. Sound should come from the direction of virtual objects or events in the AR scene.

User Interface (UI) Design

AR applications often include user interfaces for interaction and information display. Design your AR UI with the following principles in mind:

- **Minimalism:** Keep AR UI elements minimal and unobtrusive. Avoid cluttering the user's view with excessive UI elements.

- **Contextual UI:** Display UI elements when and where they are needed. Use proximity or user gaze to trigger UI displays.

- **Gestural Interfaces:** Leverage gestures for UI interaction when appropriate. Swipe, pinch, and tap gestures can enhance user engagement.

Performance Optimization

AR applications must run smoothly to maintain immersion. Performance optimization is crucial:

- **Frame Rate:** Maintain a stable frame rate (e.g., 60 frames per second) to prevent motion sickness and ensure a smooth AR experience.

- **Asset Optimization:** Compress and optimize 3D models, textures, and other assets to reduce load times and memory usage.

- **Battery Efficiency:** AR applications can be power-intensive. Optimize code and rendering to minimize battery drain.

Accessibility

Ensure that your AR experiences are accessible to a wide range of users:

- **Text and Voice Feedback:** Provide textual or voice feedback for important information. Not all users may be able to see visual cues.

- **Consider Physical Limitations:** Design interactions that accommodate users with physical limitations, such as mobility impairments.

Privacy and Security

AR applications may collect and process user data. Prioritize user privacy and security:

- **Permissions:** Clearly explain why the app needs access to certain device features, such as the camera or location.

- **Data Protection:** Implement robust data protection measures to safeguard user data from unauthorized access.

- **Data Minimization:** Collect and retain only the data necessary for the AR experience, and delete it when no longer needed.

User Testing

User testing is invaluable for refining the AR user experience. Conduct usability tests with real users to gather feedback and identify areas for improvement. Iterate on your AR application based on user insights and observations.

By considering these AR user experience considerations and implementing best practices, you can create AR applications that captivate users and deliver immersive and enjoyable experiences. Prioritizing UX enhances user engagement and ensures the success of your AR projects.

11.5 Challenges and Best Practices in Audio-Visual Integration

Integrating audio and visual elements effectively is a crucial aspect of creating immersive Augmented Reality (AR) experiences using Three.js. In this section, we will discuss the challenges and best practices in audio-visual integration to ensure that the combination of sight and sound enhances the user's AR experience.

Synchronizing Audio with Visuals

One of the primary challenges in audio-visual integration is ensuring that audio elements are perfectly synchronized with visual elements. To achieve synchronization, consider the following best practices:

- **Frame-Accurate Timing:** Ensure that audio events and visual animations are triggered with frame-accurate timing to avoid lag or desynchronization.

- **Preloading Assets:** Preload audio files and textures to minimize loading delays, ensuring that audio and visuals start together.

- **Event-Based Triggering:** Use event-based triggers to synchronize audio and visual elements. For example, play a sound when a virtual button is pressed.

Spatial Audio for Realism

Spatial audio enhances the sense of presence in AR experiences by simulating the direction and distance of sound sources in relation to the user. Here are some considerations:

- **Positional Audio:** Implement positional audio so that sound sources appear to come from the direction of virtual objects. This helps users locate and interact with AR elements based on sound cues.

- **Head-Tracking:** Utilize head-tracking data to adjust the perceived location of sound sources as the user moves. This maintains the illusion of sound coming from fixed points in the AR environment.

Audio User Interface (UI)

AR applications often include audio user interfaces (UI) to provide feedback, instructions, or information. Designing effective audio UI is essential:

- **Clarity:** Ensure that audio instructions and feedback are clear and easy to understand. Use professional voice actors or clear synthetic voices.

- **Feedback Sounds:** Provide audio feedback for user interactions, such as button presses or menu selections. These sounds should be subtle and non-disruptive.

- **Volume Control:** Allow users to control audio volume within the AR application to adapt to their environment and preferences.

Multimodal Interactions

To enhance the user experience, consider combining visual and audio cues for interactions:

- **Visual-Audio Pairing:** When a virtual object emits a sound, synchronize it with a visual effect, such as a glowing outline or animation, to reinforce the interaction.

- **Cross-Modal Feedback:** Use audio cues to reinforce visual cues and vice versa. For example, when a user selects an AR button, provide both a visual highlight and a corresponding sound.

Accessibility

Accessibility is a critical consideration in audio-visual integration:

- **Subtitle and Captioning:** If your AR application includes spoken content, provide subtitles or captioning for users with hearing impairments.

- **Audio Descriptions:** For users with visual impairments, provide audio descriptions of important visual elements and actions in the AR environment.

- **Customization:** Allow users to customize audio-visual settings to accommodate individual accessibility needs and preferences.

Performance Optimization

Efficiently managing audio-visual resources is essential for smooth AR experiences:

- **Audio Compression:** Compress audio files to reduce file sizes and minimize latency when loading and playing sounds.

- **Resource Management:** Implement resource management strategies to ensure that audio and visual assets are loaded and unloaded efficiently based on the user's interaction and location within the AR scene.

- **Cross-Platform Compatibility:** Test audio-visual integration across different AR-capable devices and platforms to ensure consistent performance and quality.

By addressing these challenges and following best practices in audio-visual integration, you can create AR experiences that captivate users and provide a seamless blend of sight and sound, resulting in truly immersive and engaging augmented reality applications.

Chapter 12: Performance Optimization

12.1 Profiling and Diagnosing Performance Issues

Performance optimization is a critical aspect of developing augmented reality (AR) applications with Three.js. To create smooth and responsive AR experiences, you need to identify and address performance bottlenecks. In this section, we'll focus on profiling and diagnosing performance issues in your AR projects.

The Importance of Performance

AR applications often push the limits of hardware and software capabilities. Users expect AR content to seamlessly blend with the real world, which requires high-performance rendering, accurate tracking, and responsive interactions. Poor performance can lead to a jarring and frustrating user experience, including issues like low frame rates, lag, or stuttering.

Profiling Tools

Profiling involves measuring and analyzing your AR application's performance to identify areas that need improvement. Several tools and techniques can help you with this process:

- **Web Browser DevTools:** Most modern web browsers offer built-in developer tools that include performance profiling features. These tools allow you to record and analyze the performance of your AR application while it runs in the browser. You can inspect CPU usage, memory consumption, and network activity.

- **Three.js Stats.js:** Three.js includes a library called Stats.js, which provides a simple overlay that displays real-time information about rendering performance, including frames per second (FPS), memory usage, and rendering time. It's a quick way to get a sense of how well your AR application is performing.

- **Performance Monitoring Services:** Consider using third-party performance monitoring services like Google's Lighthouse or New Relic. These services can provide detailed insights into your application's performance and suggest improvements.

Performance Metrics

When profiling your AR application, focus on key performance metrics:

- **Frame Rate:** Frame rate measures how many frames per second your application can render. Aim for a stable frame rate of 60 FPS, especially in AR, to ensure a smooth and immersive experience. Frame rate drops below 30 FPS can be noticeable and negatively impact user engagement.

- **CPU Usage:** Monitor CPU usage to identify tasks that consume significant processing power. Heavy computations, complex physics simulations, or inefficient rendering code can strain the CPU.

- **Memory Usage:** Keep an eye on memory usage to prevent memory leaks and excessive resource consumption. Large textures, 3D models, or inefficient asset loading can contribute to high memory usage.

- **Network Activity:** If your AR application relies on remote assets or data, monitor network activity. Slow or excessive network requests can lead to delays in content loading.

Common Performance Issues

Understanding common performance issues is essential for effective profiling and diagnosis:

- **Overly Complex 3D Models:** High-poly 3D models can be resource-intensive to render. Optimize or simplify models where possible.

- **Inefficient Asset Loading:** Loading large textures or 3D models all at once can cause delays. Implement progressive loading or streaming techniques to load assets dynamically as needed.

- **Lack of GPU Acceleration:** Ensure that your AR application leverages hardware acceleration provided by the GPU. Three.js is designed to utilize WebGL for efficient rendering.

- **Uncached Assets:** Failure to cache assets locally can lead to unnecessary downloads and delays when reopening the application.

Profiling Workflow

To effectively profile and diagnose performance issues, follow these steps:

1. **Set Baselines:** Establish performance baselines for your

AR application when it's running smoothly. Record metrics like frame rate, CPU usage, and memory usage during normal operation.

2. **Reproduce Issues:** Reproduce performance issues or bottlenecks in your AR application while profiling. This may involve complex interactions, specific scenes, or loading scenarios.
3. **Profile and Analyze:** Use profiling tools to record and analyze performance data while the AR application is running in the problematic scenario. Look for spikes in CPU usage, memory leaks, or frame rate drops.
4. **Identify Bottlenecks:** Pinpoint the specific areas or functions of your code that are causing performance issues. Isolate the bottlenecks and prioritize them based on their impact on the user experience.
5. **Optimize:** Once you've identified performance bottlenecks, implement optimizations. This may involve code refactoring, asset optimization, or reducing unnecessary computations.
6. **Test Iteratively:** After implementing optimizations, test your AR application again to ensure that the changes have improved performance. Iterate on the optimization process until you achieve the desired performance levels.

Case Study: Optimizing 3D Models

Here's a simplified example of optimizing a 3D model in Three.js to improve performance:

```
// Original high-poly 3D model

const highPolyModel = new THREE.Mesh(

new THREE.BoxGeometry(10, 10, 10),
```

```
new THREE.MeshStandardMaterial({ color: 0xff0000 })
);
// Optimized low-poly 3D model
const lowPolyModel = new THREE.Mesh(
new THREE.BoxGeometry(5, 5, 5), // Use a simpler geometry
new THREE.MeshStandardMaterial({ color: 0xff0000 })
);
```

In this example, we've replaced a high-poly 3D model with a simpler, low-poly version, which can significantly improve rendering performance.

Conclusion

Profiling and diagnosing performance issues are crucial steps in creating high-quality AR applications. By monitoring key performance metrics, understanding common issues, and following a systematic profiling workflow, you can optimize your AR projects to deliver smooth and engaging user experiences. Remember that performance optimization is an ongoing process, and continuous testing and refinement are essential to maintaining a high level of performance.

12.2 Efficient Use of Memory and Resources

Efficient memory and resource management are essential for developing augmented reality (AR) applications with Three.js. In this section, we will explore best practices for optimizing memory usage and resource management to ensure that your AR experiences run smoothly and efficiently.

Memory Considerations

AR applications often involve complex 3D models, textures, and audio assets. Inefficient memory management can lead to performance issues and crashes. Here are some memory-related best practices:

- **Texture Compression:** Use texture compression formats like JPEG or PNG for textures to reduce memory usage. Consider using texture atlases to combine multiple textures into a single image.

- **Texture Resolutions:** Avoid using excessively high-resolution textures unless necessary. Use lower resolution textures for objects that are not viewed up close.

- **Garbage Collection:** Minimize the use of JavaScript objects that trigger frequent garbage collection. Garbage collection can introduce pauses and affect performance. Reuse objects where possible.

- **Memory Profiling:** Use memory profiling tools to identify memory leaks and inefficient memory usage patterns in your AR application. Regularly monitor memory consumption during development.

Resource Loading and Unloading

Efficiently loading and unloading resources is crucial for managing memory and performance:

- **Resource Preloading:** Load essential assets during the AR application's initialization to ensure they are available when needed. Preloading can reduce delays when users interact with AR elements.

- **Resource Caching:** Cache loaded resources in memory to avoid redundant requests and improve loading times. Implement a caching strategy that balances memory usage and resource availability.

- **Lazy Loading:** Implement lazy loading for non-essential assets. Load assets dynamically as users interact with AR content to minimize initial load times.

Asset Optimization

Optimizing 3D models and assets can significantly reduce memory usage and improve rendering performance:

- **Polygon Reduction:** Use software or tools to reduce the polygon count of 3D models while preserving visual quality. Lower-poly models are more memory-efficient.

- **Texture Atlas:** Combine multiple textures into a single texture atlas to reduce the number of texture swaps during rendering, improving performance.

- **Level of Detail (LOD):** Implement LOD techniques to switch to lower-detail 3D models when objects are distant from the camera. This reduces the rendering workload.

- **Texture Formats:** Choose appropriate texture formats (e.g., JPEG, PNG, or WebP) based on the content. Use formats with a good balance between quality and compression.

Resource Management Libraries

Consider using resource management libraries and frameworks to simplify memory and resource management in your AR application:

- **THREE.LoaderUtils:** Three.js provides the THREE.LoaderUtils class, which can help with loading and caching textures and models efficiently.

- **Asset Management Libraries:** Explore third-party asset management libraries that offer features like asset loading, caching, and resource management.

Garbage Collection Optimization

Efficiently managing garbage collection in JavaScript is essential for maintaining a smooth AR experience:

- **Object Pools:** Use object pools to reuse frequently created and destroyed objects, such as bullets or particles, instead of constantly creating new ones.

- **Minimize Anonymous Functions:** Avoid creating anonymous functions within loops or event listeners, as they can lead to additional objects that require garbage collection.

- **Avoid Circular References:** Be cautious of circular references in your code, as they can prevent objects from being garbage collected. Remove references when objects are no longer needed.

Memory Constraints on Mobile Devices

Keep in mind that mobile devices, which are commonly used for AR experiences, have limited memory compared to desktop computers. Optimizing memory usage is especially crucial for AR applications on mobile platforms.

Conclusion

Efficiently managing memory and resources is essential for creating high-performance augmented reality applications with Three.js. By following best practices for memory optimization, resource loading and unloading, asset optimization, and garbage collection, you can ensure that your AR experiences run smoothly, even on devices with limited resources. Regular profiling and testing are essential to identify and address memory-related issues during development and deliver a seamless AR user experience.

12.3 Optimizing Render Loops

Optimizing the render loop of your augmented reality (AR) application is a critical step in achieving smooth and responsive AR experiences. In this section, we will explore various techniques and best practices for optimizing the render loop when using Three.js for AR development.

Understanding the Render Loop

The render loop is the heart of any graphical application, including AR experiences. It is responsible for continuously rendering frames, updating animations, and responding to user interactions. A poorly optimized render loop can lead to performance bottlenecks and a subpar user experience.

RequestAnimationFrame

In web-based AR applications using Three.js, the requestAnimationFrame method is commonly used to create the render loop. It ensures that the browser requests the next animation frame, aligning the rendering with the device's refresh rate. Here's a basic structure of a render loop:

```
function animate() {

// Update animations and game logic here

// Render the scene

renderer.render(scene, camera);

// Request the next frame

requestAnimationFrame(animate);

}

// Start the render loop

animate();
```

Frame Rate Target

Aim to maintain a consistent frame rate for your AR application. A frame rate of 60 frames per second (FPS) is ideal for delivering a smooth and immersive experience. To achieve this:

- Optimize your rendering code to ensure that it can render a frame in under 16.67 milliseconds (1 second divided by 60).

• Use performance profiling tools to identify rendering bottlenecks and optimize them.

Efficient Rendering

Efficient rendering is crucial for AR applications. Here are some rendering-related optimizations:

• **Frustum Culling:** Implement frustum culling to prevent rendering objects that are outside the camera's view frustum. This can significantly reduce the number of objects rendered in each frame.

• **Level of Detail (LOD):** Use LOD techniques to render high-detail models when they are close to the camera and lower-detail models when they are distant. This can improve rendering performance without sacrificing visual quality.

• **Batching:** Combine multiple objects with the same material and properties into a single geometry or buffer geometry. This reduces the number of draw calls and improves rendering performance.

• **Shader Optimization:** Optimize custom shaders for your AR effects. Eliminate unnecessary calculations and use GPU-friendly techniques to reduce rendering time.

Responsive User Input

Ensure that user interactions are responsive even during rendering. To achieve this:

• Use a separate event loop or thread for handling user input to prevent input lag caused by the main render loop.

• Implement frame throttling for user input updates to avoid overwhelming the application with input events.

Occlusion Culling

In AR applications, occlusion culling can be a performance-saving technique. It involves determining which objects are occluded or hidden by other objects in the scene and skipping their rendering. Implementing occlusion culling can significantly reduce the rendering workload, especially in scenes with complex 3D models.

Frame Rate Adaption

Consider implementing frame rate adaptation mechanisms. In situations where maintaining a consistent 60 FPS is challenging, dynamically adjust the frame rate based on device capabilities and scene complexity. Lower the frame rate when necessary to maintain a smooth experience without dropping too many frames.

Efficient Asset Loading

Efficiently loading and managing assets can impact the render loop's performance. Implement techniques such as asset streaming and prioritization to load and display essential assets first while deferring non-essential assets until later.

Profiling and Testing

Regularly profile your AR application's render loop to identify performance bottlenecks. Use browser developer tools and third-party profiling tools to analyze frame times, CPU usage, and memory usage. Conduct real-world testing on various devices to ensure optimal performance across different hardware configurations.

Conclusion

Optimizing the render loop of your AR application is vital for delivering a smooth and responsive user experience. By following best practices such as maintaining a consistent frame rate, implementing efficient rendering techniques, considering occlusion culling, and optimizing asset loading, you can create AR experiences that run seamlessly on a variety of devices and provide users with engaging and immersive interactions. Continuous testing, profiling, and refinement are essential to achieving optimal performance in AR applications.

12.4 Balancing Quality and Performance

Balancing quality and performance is a critical consideration when developing augmented reality (AR) applications with Three.js. Striking the right balance ensures that your AR experiences provide visually appealing content while running smoothly on a variety of devices. In this section, we'll explore strategies and best practices for achieving this balance.

Device Variability

AR applications can run on a wide range of devices, from high-end smartphones to less powerful tablets and older models. To deliver a consistent user experience, consider the following:

- **Device Capabilities:** Detect and adapt to the capabilities of the user's device. Adjust rendering settings, texture resolutions, and complexity based on available hardware resources.

- **Fallback Options:** Provide fallback options for users with lower-end devices. For example, you can offer reduced graphics quality settings to improve performance on less capable hardware.

Dynamic Quality Settings

Implement dynamic quality settings that adapt to the current device's capabilities and the complexity of the AR scene. Here are some strategies:

- **Auto-Detect Performance:** Use device feature detection and benchmarking to determine the device's performance level. Adjust rendering settings accordingly.

- **Quality Presets:** Create predefined quality presets (e.g., "low," "medium," and "high") that users can choose from based on their preferences and device capabilities.

- **User-Defined Settings:** Allow users to customize graphics settings, such as texture quality, antialiasing, and shadow quality, to balance quality and performance according to their preferences.

LOD (Level of Detail) Techniques

Level of Detail (LOD) techniques optimize rendering performance by using lower-detail versions of 3D models when objects are distant from the camera. Implement LOD strategies to:

- **Reduce Rendering Complexity:** Switch to lower-poly models or simplified textures for distant objects.

- **Improve Frame Rate:** Decrease the rendering workload, especially in scenes with many objects.

- **Maintain Visual Quality:** Ensure that objects look visually consistent even when using lower-detail LOD versions.

Streaming and Progressive Loading

Optimize asset loading by implementing streaming and progressive loading techniques:

- **Streaming:** Load essential assets first and stream additional assets as the AR application runs. This minimizes initial loading times and allows users to interact with content more quickly.

- **Progressive Loading:** Load textures and 3D models progressively, starting with lower-resolution versions and gradually increasing detail. This provides a smooth user experience while assets continue to load in the background.

Quality-Performance Trade-offs

Understand the trade-offs between quality and performance in different aspects of AR development:

- **Texture Compression:** Use texture compression formats to reduce memory usage but be aware that compression may result in some loss of texture quality.

- **Antialiasing:** Enable antialiasing for smoother edges on rendered objects, but be mindful of its impact on performance.

- **Shadow Quality:** Adjust shadow quality settings to balance realism with rendering speed. Lower-quality shadows can significantly improve performance.

- **Post-Processing Effects:** Evaluate the necessity of post-processing effects like bloom, motion blur, or depth of field. These effects can enhance visuals but may require additional GPU resources.

Continuous Testing

Regularly test your AR application on a variety of devices with different hardware configurations. This ensures that the quality-performance balance remains optimal for a broad user base. Conduct real-world performance testing to identify potential bottlenecks and address them early in development.

User Feedback

Encourage user feedback and provide a mechanism for users to report performance issues. User feedback can help you identify specific devices or scenarios where performance optimization may be needed and prioritize improvements accordingly.

Conclusion

Balancing quality and performance is an ongoing challenge in AR application development. By implementing dynamic quality settings, LOD techniques, streaming, and progressive loading, you can optimize your AR experiences to provide both visual appeal and smooth performance on a wide range of devices. Continuous testing, user feedback, and monitoring of hardware advancements are essential to maintaining this delicate balance and delivering compelling AR applications that engage and captivate users.

12.5 Best Practices for Scalable 3D Web Applications

Developing scalable 3D web applications, including augmented reality (AR) experiences with Three.js, requires careful consideration of architecture, performance, and user engagement. In this section, we will explore best practices to ensure that your AR application can scale effectively to meet growing demands and maintain a high-quality user experience.

Modular Code Structure

Adopt a modular code structure that promotes maintainability and scalability. Use techniques like component-based architecture to break down your AR application into reusable and independent modules. This allows for easier updates, code sharing, and collaboration among developers.

```
// Example of a component-based structure in Three.js

class ARObject {

constructor() {

// Initialize object properties and behavior

}

update() {
```

```
// Update object's behavior and properties
}
render() {
// Render the object in the AR scene
}
}
const arObject1 = new ARObject();
const arObject2 = new ARObject();
// Add objects to the scene
scene.add(arObject1);
scene.add(arObject2);
```

Load Balancing

For AR applications with significant server-side components, implement load balancing to distribute incoming requests and traffic across multiple servers or instances. Load balancing ensures that your application can handle increased user demand while maintaining responsiveness.

Content Delivery Networks (CDNs)

Leverage Content Delivery Networks (CDNs) to efficiently deliver static assets, such as 3D models, textures, and scripts. CDNs reduce the load on your server and provide low-latency content delivery to users worldwide. Ensure that your AR application's assets are optimized for CDNs.

Caching Strategies

Implement caching strategies to reduce the load on your server and improve response times. Use HTTP caching headers for assets that don't change frequently. Employ client-side caching techniques to store data locally on the user's device, reducing the need for repeated downloads.

Database Scalability

If your AR application relies on a database for storing and retrieving user-generated content, consider database scalability options. Use NoSQL databases or distributed database systems that can scale horizontally to accommodate increasing data volumes and user interactions.

Asynchronous Processing

Optimize server-side operations by implementing asynchronous processing. Use techniques like message queues and worker threads to offload resource-intensive tasks, such as asset processing or real-time data updates, to separate processes. This ensures that the main application remains responsive.

```
// Example of asynchronous processing with Node.js and RabbitMQ

const amqp = require('amqplib');

async function processTask(task) {

// Process the task asynchronously

}

async function startWorker() {
```

```
const connection = await amqp.connect('amqp://localhost');

const channel = await connection.createChannel();

const queue = 'tasks';

channel.assertQueue(queue, { durable: false });

console.log('Worker is waiting for tasks...');

channel.consume(queue, async (message) => {

const task = JSON.parse(message.content.toString());

await processTask(task);

channel.ack(message);

});

}

startWorker();
```

Scalable Hosting

Choose a hosting solution that can easily scale based on demand. Cloud hosting providers like AWS, Google Cloud, and Azure offer auto-scaling capabilities that automatically adjust resources to handle increased traffic. Monitor server performance and scale up or down as needed.

User Authentication and Authorization

Implement robust user authentication and authorization mechanisms to secure your AR application. Utilize OAuth, JWT (JSON Web Tokens), or other authentication protocols to protect user data and ensure that only authorized users can access certain features.

Monitoring and Analytics

Deploy monitoring and analytics tools to gain insights into your AR application's performance and user behavior. Tools like Google Analytics, New Relic, or custom telemetry solutions can help you track user engagement, identify performance bottlenecks, and make informed decisions for optimization.

Continuous Optimization

Scalability is an ongoing process. Continuously monitor your AR application, collect user feedback, and analyze performance metrics. Regularly review and optimize code, databases, and server configurations to ensure that your application remains scalable and provides an excellent user experience.

Conclusion

Building scalable 3D web applications, including AR experiences with Three.js, requires careful planning and adherence to best practices. By adopting a modular code structure, implementing load balancing, leveraging CDNs, employing caching strategies, and optimizing database scalability, you can create AR applications that can handle increasing user demand. Additionally, focusing on user authentication, monitoring, and continuous optimization will contribute to the long-term success and scalability of your AR project.

Chapter 13: Integrating with Front-End Frameworks

13.1 Using Three.js with React

Integrating Three.js with front-end frameworks like React has become a common practice for building interactive 3D web applications. React provides a structured way to manage the user interface (UI), while Three.js handles 3D rendering. In this section, we'll explore how to use Three.js with React and share best practices for a seamless integration.

Setting Up the Environment

To get started with Three.js in a React project, follow these steps:

1. **Create a React App:** Set up a new React project using tools like Create React App or your preferred React boilerplate.
2. **Install Three.js:** Add the Three.js library to your project using npm or yarn.

```
npm install three

yarn add three
```

1. **Import Three.js:** Import Three.js components and classes in your React components as needed.

```
import { Scene, PerspectiveCamera, WebGLRenderer }
from 'three';
```

Building a Three.js Component

Create a custom React component that encapsulates your Three.js scene. This component can manage the 3D scene, camera, and rendering loop.

```
import React, { useEffect, useRef } from 'react';

import { Scene, PerspectiveCamera, WebGLRenderer } from 'three';

function ThreeScene() {

const canvasRef = useRef(null);

useEffect(() => {

const scene = new Scene();

const camera = new PerspectiveCamera(75, window.innerWidth / window.innerHeight, 0.1, 1000);

const renderer = new WebGLRenderer({ canvas: canvasRef.current });

// Set up your 3D scene here (add objects, lights, etc.)

// Render loop

const animate = () => {

// Update 3D objects/animations here

renderer.render(scene, camera);

requestAnimationFrame(animate);

};

animate();
```

```
return () => {
// Clean up resources (e.g., remove event listeners)
};
}, []);
return <canvas ref={canvasRef} />;
}
export default ThreeScene;
```

Integrating React Components

You can integrate your Three.js component into your React application just like any other React component.

```
import React from 'react';
import ThreeScene from './ThreeScene';
function App() {
return (
<div className="App">
<h1>My 3D React App</h1>
<ThreeScene />
</div>
);
}
```

```
export default App;
```

Handling Events

To handle user interactions or events in your 3D scene, you can use React's event handling system. For example, you can add event listeners to your component and update the Three.js scene accordingly.

```
import React, { useEffect, useRef } from 'react';

import { Scene, PerspectiveCamera, WebGLRenderer } from 'three';

function ThreeScene() {

const canvasRef = useRef(null);

useEffect(() => {

const scene = new Scene();

const camera = new PerspectiveCamera(75, window.innerWidth / window.innerHeight, 0.1, 1000);

const renderer = new WebGLRenderer({ canvas: canvasRef.current });

// Add event listeners

window.addEventListener('resize', handleResize);

// Handle window resize

function handleResize() {

const newWidth = window.innerWidth;

const newHeight = window.innerHeight;
```

```
camera.aspect = newWidth / newHeight;

camera.updateProjectionMatrix();

renderer.setSize(newWidth, newHeight);

}

// Clean up event listeners

return () => {

window.removeEventListener('resize', handleResize);

};

}, []);

return <canvas ref={canvasRef} />;

}

export default ThreeScene;
```

State Management

React's state management is useful for controlling the dynamic behavior of your 3D scene. You can use state to update the position, scale, or appearance of 3D objects based on user input or other application logic.

```
import React, { useEffect, useRef, useState } from 'react';

import { Scene, PerspectiveCamera, WebGLRenderer, BoxGeometry, MeshBasicMaterial, Mesh } from 'three';

function ThreeScene() {

const canvasRef = useRef(null);
```

```
const [rotation, setRotation] = useState({ x: 0, y: 0 });

useEffect(() => {

const scene = new Scene();

const camera = new PerspectiveCamera(75, window.innerWidth /
window.innerHeight, 0.1, 1000);

const renderer = new WebGLRenderer({ canvas: canvasRef.current
});

const box = new Mesh(new BoxGeometry(), new
MeshBasicMaterial({ color: 0x00ff00 }));

scene.add(box);

// Update object rotation based on state

box.rotation.x = rotation.x;

box.rotation.y = rotation.y;

// Render loop

const animate = () => {

renderer.render(scene, camera);

requestAnimationFrame(animate);

};

animate();

}, [rotation]);

return (
```

```
<div>

<canvas ref={canvasRef} />

<button onClick={() => setRotation({ x: rotation.x + 0.1, y: rotation.y + 0.1 })}>Rotate</button>

</div>

);

}

export default ThreeScene;
```

React Three Fiber

Another approach to integrating Three.js with React is to use libraries like React Three Fiber, which provides a declarative and component-based way to work with Three.js. React Three Fiber simplifies the setup and management of 3D scenes and objects in a React application.

```
import React, { useRef } from 'react';

import { Canvas, useFrame } from 'react-three-fiber';

function Box() {

const meshRef = useRef();

useFrame(() => {

meshRef.current.rotation.x += 0.01;

meshRef.current.rotation.y +=
```

13.2 Three.js in Angular Applications

Integrating Three.js into Angular applications allows you to create interactive 3D experiences within the Angular framework. In this section, we will explore how to use Three.js in Angular and discuss best practices for a seamless integration.

Setting Up an Angular Project

Before integrating Three.js into your Angular application, you need to set up an Angular project. You can use the Angular CLI (Command Line Interface) to create a new project:

```
ng new my-threejs-app
```

Follow the prompts to configure your project and choose the necessary options. Once your project is created, navigate to its directory:

```
cd my-threejs-app
```

Installing Three.js

You can add the Three.js library to your Angular project using npm or yarn. Open a terminal window and run one of the following commands:

```
npm install three
```

```
yarn add three
```

Creating a Three.js Component

To integrate Three.js into an Angular component, you can create a custom Angular component that encapsulates your Three.js scene and logic.

1. Generate a new component using the Angular CLI:

```
ng generate component my-threejs
```

1. In the generated component files (e.g., my-threejs.component.ts, my-threejs.component.html, and my-threejs.component.css), you can set up your Three.js scene and rendering logic.

```
// my-threejs.component.ts

import { Component, ElementRef, OnInit, ViewChild } from '@angular/core';

import * as THREE from 'three';

@Component({

selector: 'app-my-threejs',

templateUrl: './my-threejs.component.html',

styleUrls: ['./my-threejs.component.css'],

})

export class MyThreejsComponent implements OnInit {

@ViewChild('rendererContainer', { static: true }) rendererContainer: ElementRef;

scene: THREE.Scene;

camera: THREE.PerspectiveCamera;
```

```
renderer: THREE.WebGLRenderer;

constructor() {}

ngOnInit() {

this.init();

}

init() {

this.scene = new THREE.Scene();

this.camera = new THREE.PerspectiveCamera(75,
window.innerWidth / window.innerHeight, 0.1, 1000);

this.renderer = new THREE.WebGLRenderer();

this.renderer.setSize(window.innerWidth,
window.innerHeight);

this.rendererContainer.nativeElement.appendChild(this.renderer.do

// Set up your 3D scene here (add objects, lights, etc.)

// Add a cube to the scene

const geometry = new THREE.BoxGeometry();

const material = new THREE.MeshBasicMaterial({
color: 0x00ff00 });

const cube = new THREE.Mesh(geometry, material);

this.scene.add(cube);
```

```
this.camera.position.z = 5;

// Render loop

const animate = () => {

requestAnimationFrame(animate);

cube.rotation.x += 0.01;

cube.rotation.y += 0.01;

this.renderer.render(this.scene, this.camera);

};

animate();

}

}

<!—my-threejs.component.html—>

<div #rendererContainer></div>
```

1. You can then include the app-my-threejs component in your Angular application's templates to display the Three.js scene.

```
<!—app.component.html—>

<div>

<h1>My Angular Three.js App</h1>
```

```
<app-my-threejs></app-my-threejs>

</div>
```

Handling Events and User Interactions

In Angular, you can handle user interactions and events within your Three.js component using Angular's event binding and template syntax. For example, you can add buttons or input fields in your Angular templates and use (click) or other event bindings to trigger actions in your Three.js scene.

```
<!—my-threejs.component.html—>

<div #rendererContainer></div>

<button (click)="rotateCube()">Rotate Cube</button>

// my-threejs.component.ts

//...

export class MyThreejsComponent implements OnInit {

//...

rotateCube() {

// Handle the rotation of the cube based on user interaction

// For example, change cube's rotation speed or direction

}

//...

}
```

Managing State with Angular Services

For more complex applications, you can use Angular services to manage the state of your Three.js scene and share data between components. Services can help organize your code and facilitate communication between different parts of your application.

```
// my-threejs-state.service.ts

import { Injectable } from '@angular/core';

@Injectable({

providedIn: 'root',

})

export class MyThreejsStateService {

rotationSpeed = 0.01;

}

// my-threejs.component.ts

import { Component, ElementRef, OnInit, ViewChild } from '@angular/core';

import * as THREE from 'three';

import { MyThreejsStateService } from './my-threejs-state.service';

@Component({

selector: 'app-my-threejs',
```

13.3 Vue.js and Three.js: A Synergistic Approach

Integrating Three.js with Vue.js can result in a powerful and interactive combination for building 3D web applications. In this section, we'll explore how to use Three.js within a Vue.js project and discuss best practices for seamless integration.

Setting Up a Vue.js Project

Before integrating Three.js into your Vue.js application, you need to set up a Vue.js project. You can use Vue CLI (Command Line Interface) to create a new project:

vue create my-vue-threejs-app

Follow the prompts to configure your project and choose the necessary options. Once your project is created, navigate to its directory:

cd my-vue-threejs-app

Installing Three.js

You can add the Three.js library to your Vue.js project using npm or yarn. Open a terminal window and run one of the following commands:

npm install three

yarn add three

Creating a Three.js Component

To integrate Three.js into a Vue.js component, you can create a custom Vue component that encapsulates your Three.js scene and logic.

1. Generate a new Vue component:

```
vue generate component MyThreejs
```

1. In the generated component files (e.g., MyThreejs.vue), set up your Three.js scene and rendering logic.

```
<!—MyThreejs.vue—>

<template>

<div ref="rendererContainer"></div>

</template>

<script>

import * as THREE from 'three';

export default {

mounted() {

this.init();

},

methods: {

init() {
```

```
this.scene = new THREE.Scene();

this.camera = new THREE.PerspectiveCamera(75,
window.innerWidth / window.innerHeight, 0.1, 1000);

this.renderer = new THREE.WebGLRenderer();

this.renderer.setSize(window.innerWidth,
window.innerHeight);

this.$refs.rendererContainer.appendChild(this.renderer.domElement

// Set up your 3D scene here (add objects, lights, etc.)

// Add a cube to the scene

const geometry = new THREE.BoxGeometry();

const material = new THREE.MeshBasicMaterial({
color: 0x00ff00 });

const cube = new THREE.Mesh(geometry, material);

this.scene.add(cube);

this.camera.position.z = 5;

// Render loop

const animate = () => {

requestAnimationFrame(animate);

cube.rotation.x += 0.01;

cube.rotation.y += 0.01;
```

```
this.renderer.render(this.scene, this.camera);

};

animate();

},

},

};

</script>
```

1. You can include the MyThreejs component in your Vue.js application's templates to display the Three.js scene.

```
<!—App.vue—>

<template>

<div id="app">

<h1>My Vue.js Three.js App</h1>

<my-threejs />

</div>

</template>

<script>

import MyThreejs from './components/MyThreejs.vue';

export default {
```

```
components: {
MyThreejs,
},
};
</script>
```

Handling Events and User Interactions

In Vue.js, you can handle user interactions and events within your Three.js component using Vue's event binding and template syntax. For example, you can add buttons or input fields in your Vue.js templates and use @click or other event bindings to trigger actions in your Three.js scene.

```
<!—MyThreejs.vue—>
<template>
<div>
<div ref="rendererContainer"></div>
<button @click="rotateCube">Rotate Cube</button>
</div>
</template>
<script>
import * as THREE from 'three';
export default {
// ...
```

```
methods: {
// ...
rotateCube() {
// Handle the rotation of the cube based on user interaction
// For example, change cube's rotation speed or direction
},
},
};
</script>
```

Managing State with VueX

For more complex applications, you can use VueX, the state management library for Vue.js, to manage the state of your Three.js scene and share data between components. VueX can help organize your code and facilitate communication between different parts of your application.

```
// store.js (VueX store module)
import Vue from 'vue';
import Vuex from 'vuex';
Vue.use(Vuex);
export default new Vuex.Store({
state: {
rotationSpeed: 0.01,
```

```
},
mutations: {
setRotationSpeed(state, speed) {
state.rotationSpeed = speed;
},
},
});
<!—MyThreejs.vue—>
<template>
<div>
<div ref="rendererContainer"></div>
<button @click="rotateCube">Rotate Cube</button>
</div>
</template>
<script>
import * as THREE from 'three';
import { mapState, mapMutations } from 'vuex';
export default {
// ...
computed: {
```

```
...mapState(['rotationSpeed']),
},
methods: {
...mapMutations(['setRotationSpeed']),
// ...
rotateCube() {
// Handle the rotation of the cube based on user interaction
// Use this.rotationSpeed to access the rotation speed from the store
// Use this.setRotationSpeed(newSpeed) to update the rotation speed in the store
},
},
};
</script>
```

Vue CLI Plugin for Three.js

There is also a Vue CLI plugin called vue-cli-plugin-three that simplifies the integration of Three.js into Vue.js projects. This plugin provides a boilerplate setup and a custom Vue component for Three.js scenes, making it even more convenient to create 3D web applications with Vue.js.

13.4 Server-Side Rendering and Three.js

Server-Side Rendering (SSR) with Three.js can be a challenging but rewarding approach to building interactive 3D web applications. SSR allows you to generate the initial HTML content on the server and then hydrate it on the client side, providing better SEO, faster initial page loads, and a more accessible user experience. In this section, we'll explore how to implement SSR with Three.js and discuss best practices.

Setting Up SSR in Your Framework

SSR can be implemented in various web frameworks, such as Next.js (for React), Nuxt.js (for Vue.js), or similar technologies for other frameworks. The specific implementation details may vary, but the overall approach is similar.

1. **Choose an SSR Framework:** If you're not already using an SSR framework, select one that aligns with your project's requirements. For example, if you're using React, consider Next.js, and if you're using Vue.js, consider Nuxt.js.
2. **Install and Configure:** Install the SSR framework and configure your project accordingly. Follow the framework's documentation for setting up SSR.
3. **Add Three.js:** Install the Three.js library in your SSR project just as you would in a regular client-side project.

npm install three

yarn add three

Managing the Three.js Scene

When implementing SSR with Three.js, you need to consider how to manage the 3D scene. Since SSR code runs on the server, you can't directly manipulate the DOM or WebGL context. Here are some strategies:

1. **Server-Side Scene Generation:** Generate a simplified version of the Three.js scene on the server side and render it to HTML canvas. You can then send the canvas image to the client, where it can be used as a static image or incorporated into the interactive Three.js scene.
2. **Hydration:** On the client side, create the full Three.js scene and replace the server-generated content with the interactive 3D scene. Use libraries like react-three-fiber for React or vue-threejs for Vue.js to facilitate hydration.
3. **Use a Headless Renderer:** Consider using headless WebGL renderers like offscreen-canvas in modern browsers or node-canvas in Node.js to render the scene on the server. This allows you to create a full Three.js scene on the server and send it to the client as a complete interactive scene.

Handling Client-Side Interactivity

Once the initial HTML with Three.js content is loaded on the client side, you can add interactivity as usual. Use the same techniques and libraries you would in a regular client-side Three.js project.

For example, you can add event listeners, animations, and user interactions just as you would in a client-side-only application. Here's an example of how you might add interactivity to a Three.js scene in a Next.js project with React:

```
// pages/index.js (Next.js page)

import { useEffect, useRef } from 'react';

import * as THREE from 'three';

export default function Home() {

const canvasRef = useRef();

useEffect(() => {

const scene = new THREE.Scene();

const camera = new THREE.PerspectiveCamera(75, window.innerWidth / window.innerHeight, 0.1, 1000);

const renderer = new THREE.WebGLRenderer({ canvas: canvasRef.current });

// Set up your Three.js scene here

camera.position.z = 5;

const animate = () => {

// Update your scene and animations here

renderer.render(scene, camera);

requestAnimationFrame(animate);

};

animate();

}, []);

return <canvas ref={canvasRef} />;
```

}

SEO Considerations

One of the main benefits of SSR is improved SEO because search engine crawlers can access the fully rendered HTML content. However, when using SSR with Three.js, you should be aware of SEO challenges:

1. **Initial Content:** SSR generates the initial HTML content, but if your Three.js scene relies on dynamic data or assets that load asynchronously, search engines may not see the complete content. Consider pre-rendering or server-side rendering the necessary data for the 3D scene.
2. **Metadata:** Ensure that you provide appropriate metadata, including titles, descriptions, and structured data, to help search engines understand the content of your SSR pages.
3. **Sitemaps and Robots.txt:** Submit sitemaps and configure your robots.txt file to guide search engines in crawling and indexing your SSR pages.
4. **Crawler-Friendly URLs:** Use clean and SEO-friendly URLs to make it easier for search engines to index your pages.

Performance Optimization

SSR can increase the time it takes to generate pages on the server compared to client-side rendering. To maintain good performance, consider the following:

1. **Caching:** Implement server-side caching to store pre-rendered pages and reduce server load. Use cache-control headers to control caching behavior.
2. **Code Splitting:** Divide your code into smaller bundles

and load only what's necessary for the current page. Code splitting helps reduce initial load times.

3. **Lazy Loading:** Lazy load

13.5 Managing State and Data Flow in Complex Applications

When building complex 3D web applications with Three.js and a front-end framework like React, Angular, or Vue.js, managing state and data flow is crucial for maintaining code maintainability and scalability. In this section, we'll explore strategies and patterns for managing state and data flow in these applications.

Component-Based State Management

In component-based front-end frameworks like React, Angular, and Vue.js, state management often starts at the component level. Each component can have its own local state to manage data specific to that component's functionality. For example, a Three.js-based component may have state variables to control the position, rotation, or visibility of 3D objects.

```
// Example React component state

import React, { useState } from 'react';

function ThreeJsComponent() {

const [rotation, setRotation] = useState(0);

// ...

return (

<div>
```

```
{/* JSX to render Three.js scene */}
</div>
);
}
```

Global State Management

In more complex applications, you may need to share state and data between components that are not directly related. To achieve this, you can use global state management solutions like React Context API, Redux, Angular services, or VueX. These libraries allow you to create a central store where you can store and retrieve shared data.

```
// Example using React Context API
import React, { createContext, useContext, useState } from 'react';
const MyContext = createContext();
function MyProvider({ children }) {
const [globalState, setGlobalState] = useState(initialState);
return (
<MyContext.Provider value={{ globalState, setGlobalState }}>
{children}
</MyContext.Provider>
);
}
function useGlobalState() {
```

```
return useContext(MyContext);

}

// Usage in components

function AnotherComponent() {

const { globalState, setGlobalState } = useGlobalState();

// Access and modify global state

}
```

Data Flow and Event Handling

When working with Three.js, you often need to update the 3D scene in response to user interactions or external events. To achieve this, you can establish clear data flow and event handling mechanisms.

- **User Interaction:** Implement event listeners for user interactions such as mouse clicks, keyboard input, or touch events. These listeners can trigger state changes or animations in the 3D scene.

```
// Example using React for mouse click interaction

function handleMouseClick() {

// Update state or trigger animations

}

return (

<div>

<button onClick={handleMouseClick}>Click me</button>
```

```
</div>
);
```

- **Data Propagation:** Pass data and state changes down to child components as props or through the context API. This ensures that changes in one component can affect the rendering or behavior of child components.

```
// Example passing state as props in React
function ParentComponent() {
const [rotation, setRotation] = useState(0);
return (
<div>
<ChildComponent rotation={rotation} />
</div>
);
}
function ChildComponent({ rotation }) {
// Use rotation in the Three.js scene
}
```

Asynchronous Data Loading

In many 3D web applications, you may need to load 3D models, textures, or other assets asynchronously. When dealing with asynchronous operations, consider using promises, async/await, or reactive programming patterns to handle data loading and ensure a smooth user experience.

```
// Example using async/await to load a 3D model in Three.js
async function loadModel() {
const loader = new THREE.GLTFLoader();
const model = await loader.loadAsync('/path/to/model.glb');
// Add the loaded model to the scene
}
```

Real-Time Communication

For applications that require real-time communication or multiplayer features, you can use technologies like WebSockets or serverless functions to exchange data and updates between clients and the server. Libraries like Socket.io or GraphQL subscriptions can facilitate real-time interactions.

```
// Example using WebSocket in a Three.js application
const socket = new WebSocket('ws://example.com/socket');
socket.addEventListener('open', (event) => {
// Send and receive real-time updates
});
socket.addEventListener('message', (event) => {
// Handle incoming messages
});
```

Testing and Debugging

Maintaining a complex 3D web application also involves thorough testing and debugging. You can use testing frameworks and tools specific to your front-end framework to ensure that your components and interactions work as expected. Additionally, browser developer tools and Three.js debugging utilities can help diagnose issues related to the 3D scene.

In summary, managing state and data flow in complex 3D web applications involves a combination of local component state, global state management, event handling, and data loading strategies. By carefully architecting your application and choosing appropriate tools and patterns, you can create maintainable and scalable 3D web experiences.

14.1 Principles of 3D Data Visualization

In Chapter 14, we delve into the exciting world of 3D data visualization using Three.js. Visualizing data in three dimensions can provide a deeper understanding of complex datasets, making it easier to identify patterns, relationships, and outliers. In this section, we'll explore the fundamental principles and concepts of 3D data visualization to lay the foundation for creating informative and engaging visualizations.

The Power of Three Dimensions

Three-dimensional data visualization adds an extra dimension of depth to your visualizations compared to traditional 2D plots or charts. This additional dimension can represent a wide range of variables or attributes, allowing you to convey more information simultaneously. Some key advantages of 3D data visualization include:

1. **Multivariate Analysis:** With three dimensions, you can visualize data with multiple variables, making it easier to explore complex relationships within the data.
2. **Spatial Context:** 3D visualizations often represent data in a spatial context, mimicking the way we perceive the physical world. This spatial context can provide a more intuitive understanding of the data.
3. **Pattern Recognition:** 3D visualizations can reveal patterns and trends that might be hidden in 2D representations. It allows you to explore data from different angles and perspectives.

Choosing the Right Visualization Type

Effective 3D data visualization starts with selecting the appropriate visualization type for your dataset and objectives. Common types of 3D visualizations include:

- **3D Scatter Plots:** These are suitable for visualizing the relationships between three continuous variables. Each data point is represented as a marker in 3D space, and the position of the marker corresponds to the values of the variables.

- **3D Surface Plots:** These visualizations are used to represent functions or relationships between two independent variables and one dependent variable. The surface represents the dependent variable, and its shape and contour lines reveal patterns.

- **3D Bar Charts:** 3D bar charts extend traditional 2D bar charts into the third dimension. They are useful for comparing values across multiple categories or variables.

- **3D Heatmaps:** These visualizations combine the concept of heatmaps with 3D space. They are suitable for representing the distribution or density of data points in three dimensions.

- **3D Line Plots:** Similar to 2D line charts, 3D line plots connect data points with lines, allowing you to visualize trends or changes in data over time or across variables.

Data Preparation and Preprocessing

Before creating a 3D data visualization, it's crucial to prepare and preprocess your data to ensure it's suitable for the chosen visualization type. Consider the following steps:

1. **Data Cleaning:** Remove any missing or inconsistent data points that could distort the visualization.
2. **Scaling and Normalization:** Scale or normalize your data if the variables have significantly different ranges. This ensures that no variable dominates the visualization.
3. **Dimensionality Reduction:** For high-dimensional datasets, consider using dimensionality reduction techniques like Principal Component Analysis (PCA) to reduce the number of variables while preserving essential information.
4. **Binning and Aggregation:** If your data is continuous, consider binning it into discrete intervals for visualization. Aggregation methods like mean, median, or sum can be applied to aggregate data within bins.
5. **Variable Mapping:** Map your data variables to the appropriate visual encoding, such as position, color, size, or shape, based on the visualization type and the insights you want to convey.

Interactivity and Exploration

Interactive 3D data visualizations empower users to explore and interact with data dynamically. Consider adding the following interactive features to your 3D visualizations:

- **Rotation and Zoom:** Allow users to rotate and zoom in/out of the 3D scene to view data from different angles and scales.

- **Hover Effects:** Provide tooltips or hover effects that display additional information when users hover over data points or elements.

- **Filtering and Selection:** Allow users to filter and select data points based on criteria or interactions. This enables focused exploration of specific subsets of the data.

- **Animations:** Use animations to highlight changes in data over time or in response to user actions. Animations can make the visualization more engaging and informative.

- **Data Exploration Controls:** Provide controls or widgets that allow users to adjust visualization parameters, such as variable mappings, color scales, or transparency levels.

Considerations for 3D Data Visualization

While 3D data visualization offers many advantages, it also comes with challenges and considerations:

- **Clutter and Occlusion:** Visual clutter can occur when there are too many data points or elements in the 3D space. Occlusion, where data points hide each other, can also be a problem. Consider techniques like transparency, data aggregation, or depth-based rendering to address these issues.

- **Color Scales:** Choose color scales carefully to ensure that data is effectively encoded. Be mindful of colorblindness considerations and choose color combinations that are accessible to all users.

- **Performance:** Complex 3D visualizations can be computationally intensive and may require optimization techniques to maintain smooth interactions and render large datasets efficiently.

- **User Guidance:** Provide clear instructions or hints to guide users in interacting with the visualization. Explain the meaning of axes, legends, and other elements.

In summary, 3D data visualization is a powerful tool for exploring and communicating complex datasets. By understanding the principles of 3D visualization, selecting the right visualization type, preparing your data, and incorporating interactivity, you can create informative and engaging 3D visualizations that reveal insights and patterns within your data.

14.2 Creating Interactive Graphs and Charts

In 3D data visualization, creating interactive graphs and charts allows you to convey complex data in a more accessible and engaging manner. Interactive visualizations enable users to explore data, gain insights, and make data-driven decisions. In this section, we'll explore how to create interactive 3D graphs and charts using Three.js and other related libraries.

Choosing the Right Graph Type

Before creating an interactive 3D graph or chart, it's essential to select the appropriate graph type that best represents your data and the insights you want to convey. Some common 3D graph types include:

- **3D Scatter Plots:** These plots are suitable for visualizing the relationships between three continuous variables. Each data point is represented as a marker in 3D space, where the position of the marker corresponds to the values of the variables.

- **3D Surface Plots:** Surface plots are used to represent functions or relationships between two independent variables and one dependent variable. The surface represents the dependent variable, and its shape and contour lines reveal patterns.

- **3D Bar Charts:** 3D bar charts extend traditional 2D bar charts into the third dimension. They are useful for comparing values across multiple categories or variables.

- **3D Heatmaps:** Heatmaps in 3D combine the concept of heatmaps with 3D space. They are suitable for representing the distribution or density of data points in three dimensions.

- **3D Line Plots:** Similar to 2D line charts, 3D line plots connect data points with lines, allowing you to visualize trends or changes in data over time or across variables.

Using Three.js for 3D Graphs

Three.js is a powerful library for creating 3D graphics and visualizations in the browser. To create interactive 3D graphs and charts, you can leverage Three.js's capabilities to render and manipulate 3D objects. Here's a basic example of how to create a simple 3D scatter plot using Three.js:

```
// Import Three.js library

import * as THREE from 'three';

// Create a scene

const scene = new THREE.Scene();

// Create a perspective camera

const camera = new THREE.PerspectiveCamera(75, window.innerWidth / window.innerHeight, 0.1, 1000);

camera.position.z = 5;

// Create a WebGLRenderer

const renderer = new THREE.WebGLRenderer();

renderer.setSize(window.innerWidth, window.innerHeight);

document.body.appendChild(renderer.domElement);

// Create data points as spheres

const dataPoints = [];

const numPoints = 100;

for (let i = 0; i < numPoints; i++) {
```

```
const sphereGeometry = new THREE.SphereGeometry(0.1, 32, 32);

const sphereMaterial = new THREE.MeshBasicMaterial({ color: 0xff0000 });

const sphere = new THREE.Mesh(sphereGeometry, sphereMaterial);

// Randomly position data points

sphere.position.x = Math.random() * 10 - 5;

sphere.position.y = Math.random() * 10 - 5;

sphere.position.z = Math.random() * 10 - 5;

dataPoints.push(sphere);

scene.add(sphere);

}

// Create an animation loop

const animate = () => {

requestAnimationFrame(animate);

// Rotate the data points

dataPoints.forEach((sphere) => {

sphere.rotation.x += 0.01;

sphere.rotation.y += 0.01;

});
```

```
renderer.render(scene, camera);

};

animate();
```

This example sets up a basic Three.js scene with a perspective camera and creates a set of randomly positioned data points represented as spheres. The animation loop continuously rotates the data points, creating a simple interactive 3D scatter plot.

Adding Interactivity

Interactivity is a key aspect of 3D graphs and charts. Users should be able to interact with the visualization to explore data and gain insights. Some common interactive features to consider include:

- **Tooltip Display:** Show tooltips with data values when users hover over data points, allowing them to inspect specific data.

- **Zoom and Pan:** Implement zooming and panning functionality to allow users to navigate the 3D space and focus on specific areas of interest.

- **Selection and Filtering:** Enable users to select data points or regions in the 3D graph to filter and explore subsets of the data.

- **Axis Controls:** Provide controls for users to change the scale and orientation of axes, allowing them to view data from different perspectives.

- **Data Highlighting:** Implement highlighting effects to emphasize specific data points or regions based on user interactions or queries.

To add these interactive features, you can use Three.js's event handling capabilities and incorporate HTML/CSS elements for tooltips and user controls.

Utilizing Charting Libraries

While Three.js is versatile for creating custom 3D visualizations, you can also leverage specialized 3D charting libraries and frameworks that simplify the creation of interactive 3D graphs and charts. Libraries like Plotly 3D, Babylon.js, or Highcharts 3D offer pre-built components and interactive features tailored for data visualization.

These libraries often provide APIs for easily creating 3D scatter plots, surface plots, bar charts, heatmaps, and more. They also include features like zooming, panning, tooltip display, and data selection out of the box, reducing the amount of custom code required.

In summary, creating interactive 3D graphs and charts involves choosing the right graph type, leveraging Three.js or specialized charting libraries, and implementing interactive features to enhance user exploration of data. By carefully designing and developing your 3D visualizations, you can provide valuable insights and an engaging user experience.

14.3 Visualizing Large Datasets

Visualizing large datasets in 3D can be a challenging but rewarding endeavor. Whether you're working with massive point clouds, volumetric data, or high-resolution 3D models, effectively visualizing and interacting with large datasets requires careful consideration of performance, scalability, and user experience. In this section, we'll explore strategies for visualizing large datasets in 3D using Three.js.

Challenges of Large Datasets

When dealing with large datasets in 3D visualization, several challenges may arise:

- **Performance:** Rendering a large number of data points or complex 3D models in real-time can strain the computational resources of the user's device, leading to slow frame rates and a subpar user experience.

- **Memory Usage:** Storing and managing large datasets in memory can be memory-intensive, and exceeding device memory limits may result in crashes or degraded performance.

- **Interactivity:** Providing smooth interactivity, such as zooming, panning, and selection, becomes challenging when dealing with large datasets.

Level of Detail (LOD)

One effective strategy for handling large datasets is using the Level of Detail (LOD) technique. LOD involves rendering simplified representations of data when zoomed out or viewing data from a distance and progressively rendering more detailed representations as the user zooms in or gets closer to the data.

In Three.js, LOD can be implemented by creating multiple versions of your 3D data, each with varying levels of detail. When rendering, you dynamically switch between these representations based on the user's viewpoint. Here's a simplified example of LOD in Three.js:

```
// Create multiple LOD levels

const lod = new THREE.LOD();

const lowDetailGeometry = new THREE.BoxGeometry(1, 1, 1);

const lowDetailMaterial = new THREE.MeshBasicMaterial({
color: 0xff0000 });

const lowDetailMesh = new THREE.Mesh(lowDetailGeometry,
lowDetailMaterial);

lowDetailMesh.scale.set(0.5, 0.5, 0.5);

const highDetailGeometry = new THREE.BoxGeometry(1, 1, 1);

const highDetailMaterial = new THREE.MeshBasicMaterial({
color: 0x00ff00 });

const highDetailMesh = new THREE.Mesh(highDetailGeometry,
highDetailMaterial);

// Add LOD levels

lod.addLevel(lowDetailMesh, 10); // Display at a distance of 10 units

lod.addLevel(highDetailMesh, 0); // Display up close

scene.add(lod);
```

In this example, a LOD container is created with two levels of detail: one with a lower detail 3D model and one with a higher detail 3D model. The LOD container automatically switches between these levels based on the camera's distance from the LOD object.

Data Streaming and Chunking

For extremely large datasets that cannot be loaded entirely into memory, data streaming and chunking can be a solution. With this approach, you load and render data in smaller, manageable chunks or tiles as needed. This technique is commonly used in geographic information systems (GIS) for rendering large maps.

In Three.js, you can implement data streaming and chunking by dynamically loading and unloading 3D models or data chunks based on the user's viewpoint and position. External data sources, such as servers or cloud storage, can provide the necessary data chunks on-demand.

GPU Instancing

GPU instancing is a technique that allows you to render multiple instances of the same 3D object with a single draw call. This can significantly improve rendering performance when you have many identical or similar objects in your scene.

In Three.js, you can leverage GPU instancing by using the THREE.InstancedMesh class. Here's a simplified example:

```
// Create a single 3D model geometry

const geometry = new THREE.BoxGeometry(1, 1, 1);

const material = new THREE.MeshBasicMaterial({ color: 0xff0000 });

// Create an instanced mesh with 1000 instances

const mesh = new THREE.InstancedMesh(geometry, material, 1000);
```

```
// Randomly position instances
for (let i = 0; i < 1000; i++) {
const matrix = new THREE.Matrix4();
matrix.makeTranslation(Math.random() * 10 - 5, Math.random() * 10 - 5, Math.random() * 10 - 5);
mesh.setMatrixAt(i, matrix);
}
scene.add(mesh);
```

In this example, a single 3D model is created, and 1000 instances of that model are rendered efficiently using GPU instancing. This technique can be particularly useful when rendering large numbers of similar objects, such as vegetation in a 3D environment.

Progressive Loading and LOD Hierarchies

For 3D models or point cloud data, you can implement progressive loading and LOD hierarchies. Instead of loading the entire model or dataset at once, you load and render portions of it progressively as the user interacts with the scene. LOD hierarchies can be used to switch between lower and higher detail representations of the data based on proximity.

Three.js provides loaders and utilities for loading 3D models and point cloud data progressively, allowing you to manage large datasets efficiently.

Culling and Frustum Optimization

Culling involves removing objects or data that are not within the camera's field of view or outside the view frustum. Implementing culling mechanisms is essential for optimizing the rendering of large datasets.

In Three.js, you can use the built-in frustum culling feature, which automatically removes objects that are not visible to the camera. Additionally, you can implement custom culling logic to further optimize the rendering of specific types of data.

Consider Web Workers

Web Workers are a technology that allows you to offload computationally intensive tasks to background threads, freeing up the main thread for rendering and user interactions. When working with large datasets, you can use Web Workers to process and prepare data asynchronously while maintaining a responsive user interface.

Web Workers can be particularly useful for tasks like data preprocessing, LOD generation, or complex calculations related to your 3D visualization.

Summary

Visualizing large datasets in 3D requires a combination of strategies and techniques to ensure performance, scalability, and a smooth user experience. These strategies include Level of Detail (LOD), data streaming and chunking, GPU instancing, progressive loading, culling, and the use of Web Workers. By carefully implementing these techniques based on the specific characteristics of your dataset, you can create impressive 3D visualizations that effectively convey information from even the largest datasets.

14.4 Using Three.js in Business Intelligence

Business Intelligence (BI) involves the use of data analysis tools and techniques to make informed decisions and gain insights into business operations. While BI traditionally relies on 2D charts and graphs, the integration of 3D visualizations using Three.js can provide a new dimension of understanding and analysis. In this section, we'll explore how Three.js can be applied in the field of Business Intelligence.

Enhancing Data Exploration

Three.js can be used to create interactive 3D visualizations that enhance data exploration in BI applications. By representing data in a 3D space, users can gain a deeper understanding of complex datasets. Here are some ways Three.js can enhance data exploration:

- **Multidimensional Analysis:** Three.js enables the visualization of multidimensional data in a single view, allowing users to explore correlations and patterns across multiple variables simultaneously.

- **Interactive Dashboards:** BI dashboards can incorporate 3D visualizations to provide users with interactive tools for drilling down into data, selecting regions of interest, and gaining insights through 3D exploration.

- **Time-Series Analysis:** 3D visualizations can be used to represent time-series data in a spatial context, enabling users to analyze trends and anomalies over time more effectively.

Visualizing Geographic Data

Geospatial analysis is a crucial component of BI, especially for businesses with location-dependent operations. Three.js can be used to create interactive 3D maps and geospatial visualizations that provide insights into geographic data. Some applications include:

- **Market Analysis:** Visualizing sales data, customer demographics, and competition in a 3D map can help businesses identify market opportunities and plan expansion strategies.

- **Logistics and Supply Chain Management:** 3D maps can be used to optimize routes, track shipments, and analyze distribution networks, improving efficiency and reducing costs.

- **Real Estate and Property Management:** 3D visualizations of properties and their surroundings can assist in property valuation, site selection, and urban planning.

Simulation and What-If Scenarios

Three.js can be applied in BI for simulating scenarios and conducting "what-if" analyses. By creating 3D models and simulations, businesses can explore different scenarios and assess the potential outcomes of various decisions. Here are some examples:

- **Financial Modeling:** Three.js can be used to visualize financial data and simulate scenarios such as investment strategies, risk analysis, and portfolio optimization.

- **Manufacturing and Operations:** Businesses can simulate production processes, warehouse layouts, and supply chain scenarios to identify bottlenecks, optimize workflows, and improve resource allocation.

- **Healthcare Analytics:** Three.js can assist in simulating patient flows, hospital layouts, and healthcare resource allocation, helping healthcare providers make informed decisions.

Collaborative Data Exploration

Collaborative BI involves multiple users working together to analyze data and make decisions. Three.js can support collaborative data exploration by enabling real-time 3D visualization sharing and interaction. Here are ways in which Three.js can facilitate collaborative BI:

- **Shared Virtual Environments:** Teams can collaborate in shared 3D environments, where multiple users interact with 3D visualizations simultaneously. This is particularly valuable for remote teams and virtual meetings.

- **Annotation and Marking:** Users can annotate and mark 3D visualizations, allowing them to highlight important insights and share comments with collaborators.

- **Data Integration:** Collaborative BI tools can integrate with Three.js to provide real-time data updates and synchronization, ensuring that all team members view the latest information.

Data Storytelling and Presentation

Data storytelling is an essential aspect of BI, as it helps communicate insights and findings effectively. Three.js can be used to create compelling data narratives by incorporating 3D visualizations into presentations and reports. Some considerations for data storytelling with Three.js include:

- **Narrative Flow:** Structure the narrative around the 3D visualizations to guide the audience through the story, explaining key findings and insights.

- **User Interaction:** Allow viewers to interact with 3D visualizations during presentations, enabling them to explore data on their terms.

- **Contextualization:** Use 3D visualizations to provide context and support key points in the narrative.

- **Accessibility:** Ensure that 3D visualizations are accessible to all viewers, including those with disabilities, by providing alternative representations and descriptions.

In summary, Three.js can be a valuable addition to the field of Business Intelligence by enhancing data exploration, visualizing geographic data, supporting simulation and what-if analyses, facilitating collaborative data exploration, and improving data storytelling and presentation. When used effectively, Three.js can provide businesses with new perspectives on their data and help them make data-driven decisions more efficiently.

14.5 Case Studies: Effective Data Visualization

In this section, we'll delve into case studies that highlight the effectiveness of data visualization using Three.js in various domains. These real-world examples demonstrate how Three.js has been applied to solve specific problems and provide valuable insights.

1. Healthcare Analytics

One compelling case involves the use of Three.js in healthcare analytics. A hospital network wanted to optimize patient flow and resource allocation. They used Three.js to create a 3D simulation of patient movements within the hospital, including waiting areas, treatment rooms, and the emergency department. This visualization allowed them to identify bottlenecks, improve staff allocation, and reduce patient waiting times. Real-time data integration enabled the hospital to make dynamic adjustments to resources based on patient influx.

```
// Sample code for creating a 3D hospital simulation using Three.js

const scene = new THREE.Scene();

const camera = new THREE.PerspectiveCamera(/*... */);

const renderer = new THREE.WebGLRenderer(/*... */);

// Create 3D models for hospital components (rooms, hallways, etc.)

const emergencyRoom = new THREE.Mesh(/*... */);

const waitingArea = new THREE.Mesh(/*... */);

const treatmentRooms = []; // Array of treatment room models
```

```
// Position and arrange models within the scene

emergencyRoom.position.set(/*... */);

waitingArea.position.set(/*... */);

// ... position and arrange treatment rooms ...

// Add models to the scene

scene.add(emergencyRoom);

scene.add(waitingArea);

// ... add treatment rooms to the scene ...

// Render the scene

renderer.render(scene, camera);
```

2. Financial Data Visualization

A financial institution wanted to provide its clients with a more intuitive way to explore their investment portfolios. They used Three.js to create a 3D representation of financial data, where each asset was visualized as a 3D object with attributes such as size, color, and height corresponding to various financial metrics. Clients could navigate their portfolios in a 3D space, making it easier to spot trends and analyze performance.

```
// Sample code for rendering financial data in 3D using Three.js

const scene = new THREE.Scene();

const camera = new THREE.PerspectiveCamera(/*... */);

const renderer = new THREE.WebGLRenderer(/*... */);
```

```
// Create 3D models for financial assets (stocks, bonds, etc.)
const stocks = []; // Array of stock models
const bonds = []; // Array of bond models
// Position and scale models based on financial data
stocks.forEach((stock) => {
stock.position.set(/*... */);
stock.scale.set(/*... */);
});
bonds.forEach((bond) => {
bond.position.set(/*... */);
bond.scale.set(/*... */);
});
// Add models to the scene
stocks.forEach((stock) => scene.add(stock));
bonds.forEach((bond) => scene.add(bond));
// Render the scene
renderer.render(scene, camera);
```

3. Urban Planning and Smart Cities

In the context of urban planning, Three.js has been employed to visualize proposed city developments and infrastructure projects. Urban planners can create 3D models of cities and simulate the impact of new construction projects, road expansions, or public transportation systems. Stakeholders and decision-makers can explore these 3D urban models to understand the consequences and benefits of various planning scenarios.

```
// Sample code for creating a 3D urban model using Three.js

const scene = new THREE.Scene();

const camera = new THREE.PerspectiveCamera(/*... */);

const renderer = new THREE.WebGLRenderer(/*... */);

// Create 3D models for buildings, roads, and infrastructure

const buildings = []; // Array of building models

const roads = []; // Array of road models

const publicTransport = []; // Array of public transport models

// Position and arrange models within the urban model

buildings.forEach((building) => {

building.position.set(/*... */);

// ... position and arrange buildings ...

});

roads.forEach((road) => {

road.position.set(/*... */);

// ... position and arrange roads ...

});
```

```
publicTransport.forEach((transport) => {
transport.position.set(/*... */);
// ... position and arrange public transport ...
});
// Add models to the scene
buildings.forEach((building) => scene.add(building));
roads.forEach((road) => scene.add(road));
publicTransport.forEach((transport) => scene.add(transport));
// Render the urban model
renderer.render(scene, camera);
```

These case studies demonstrate the versatility of Three.js in various domains, including healthcare analytics, financial data visualization, and urban planning. By harnessing the power of 3D visualizations, organizations can gain deeper insights, optimize processes, and enhance decision-making across a wide range of industries.

15.1 Basics of WebSockets and Real-Time Communication

WebSockets are a fundamental technology for enabling real-time communication between a client (typically a web browser) and a server. In the context of Three.js and 3D web applications, WebSockets play a crucial role in creating multiplayer experiences, synchronizing data across clients, and enabling interactive and collaborative 3D environments. In this section, we'll explore the basics of WebSockets and their relevance to real-time 3D web applications.

Understanding WebSockets

WebSockets provide a full-duplex communication channel over a single TCP connection, allowing bidirectional data exchange between a client and a server. Unlike traditional HTTP requests, which are stateless and involve one-time requests and responses, WebSockets establish a persistent, low-latency connection that remains open as long as needed.

Key characteristics of WebSockets include:

- **Real-Time:** WebSockets enable real-time, low-latency communication, making them ideal for applications that require instant updates and interactivity.

- **Efficient:** WebSocket connections are efficient in terms of both bandwidth and server resources because they eliminate the need for frequent HTTP polling.

- **Full-Duplex:** With WebSockets, both the client and server can send data independently and concurrently, allowing for bi-directional communication.

- **Standardized:** WebSockets are based on a standardized protocol, making them widely supported across modern web browsers and server frameworks.

WebSocket Protocol

WebSockets use a specific protocol that differs from HTTP. The WebSocket protocol starts with an HTTP handshake but then upgrades to the WebSocket protocol, transitioning to a persistent and full-duplex connection. Here's a simplified overview of the WebSocket handshake process:

1. The client sends an HTTP request to the server, including a special header indicating its desire to establish a WebSocket connection.
2. If the server supports WebSockets, it responds with an HTTP 101 status code, indicating the switching of protocols to WebSocket.
3. Once the connection is established, both the client and server can send WebSocket frames containing data back and forth.

Use Cases in Three.js

WebSockets are invaluable for enhancing interactivity and real-time features in Three.js applications:

1. **Multiplayer Games:** WebSockets enable real-time multiplayer gaming experiences where players can interact with each other in a shared 3D environment. Game state, player actions, and updates can be efficiently synchronized across all clients.
2. **Collaborative Environments:** In collaborative 3D environments, such as virtual meetings or design sessions, WebSockets allow multiple users to interact with and manipulate 3D objects together in real time.
3. **Live Data Streams:** WebSockets can be used to stream live data into a 3D visualization. For example, in a data visualization dashboard, WebSocket connections can feed real-time data updates for dynamic visualizations.
4. **3D Chat and Communication:** In virtual worlds or social VR experiences, WebSockets facilitate real-time chat, voice

communication, and presence information.

WebSocket Libraries for Three.js

When implementing WebSockets in Three.js applications, you can leverage WebSocket libraries that simplify the process. Some popular WebSocket libraries for JavaScript include:

- Socket.IO[2]: A widely used library that simplifies WebSocket implementation and provides features like automatic reconnection and rooms for managing multiple channels of communication.

- WebSocket-Node[3]: A WebSocket library for Node.js that can be used on the server side to establish WebSocket connections with clients.

- uWebSocket.js[4]: An efficient WebSocket library for Node.js that boasts high performance and low overhead.

In summary, WebSockets are a fundamental technology for enabling real-time communication in Three.js and 3D web applications. Understanding the WebSocket protocol, its advantages, and its use cases in Three.js can open up exciting possibilities for creating interactive and collaborative 3D experiences that respond in real time to user actions and data updates.

15.2 Building a Multiplayer Environment

Creating a multiplayer environment in a Three.js application involves implementing real-time communication between multiple

2. https://socket.io/

3. https://github.com/theturtle32/WebSocket-Node

4. https://github.com/uNetworking/uWebSockets.js

clients (players) and the server. This enables players to interact with each other within the shared 3D space, making multiplayer games, collaborative simulations, and social VR experiences possible. In this section, we'll explore the essential components and steps required to build a multiplayer environment using WebSockets and Three.js.

Components of a Multiplayer Environment

1. **Server:** The server acts as the central authority in a multiplayer environment. It manages game state, player connections, and communication between clients. The server is responsible for sending and receiving messages to and from clients, keeping the game synchronized.
2. **Client:** Each player's device (typically a web browser) runs a client that communicates with the server. Clients handle user input, render the 3D scene, and update the game based on server messages and player actions.
3. **Game State:** The game state represents the current state of the multiplayer environment, including the positions and actions of all players, objects, and entities in the 3D world. The server maintains the authoritative game state.
4. **Networking Protocol:** A custom or standardized networking protocol (often using WebSockets) facilitates communication between clients and the server. Messages can include player positions, actions, chat messages, and more.

Steps to Build a Multiplayer Environment

Building a multiplayer environment in Three.js involves the following steps:

1. **Set Up the Server:** Create a server application using a

server-side technology like Node.js. Implement WebSocket support using a library like Socket.IO or WebSocket-Node.
2. **Initialize the Three.js Scene:** Set up the 3D scene on the client-side using Three.js. Load models, create player avatars, and configure the rendering environment.
3. **WebSocket Connection:** Establish a WebSocket connection from the client to the server. Upon connection, the server should assign a unique identifier to each client (e.g., a player ID).
4. **Player Movement:** Capture user input on the client side (keyboard, mouse, or gamepad) to control the player's movement and actions. Transmit player input as WebSocket messages to the server.
5. **Server-Client Communication:** Implement communication between the server and clients to exchange game state updates. Clients should send their input, and the server should broadcast these inputs to all other clients, ensuring synchronization.
6. **Game Logic:** On the server, implement the game logic to process player input, update the game state, and send the updated state to all clients. This includes handling collisions, physics, and any game-specific mechanics.
7. **Synchronization:** Ensure that all clients receive and apply game state updates from the server in real time. Use interpolation and extrapolation techniques to smooth out movement and prevent jitter.
8. **Chat and Interaction:** Implement chat functionality and interactions between players. Allow players to send messages, trigger actions, and collaborate within the 3D environment.
9. **Security Measures:** Implement security measures to prevent cheating and unauthorized access. Validate player

input on the server to ensure fair gameplay.

10. **Scaling:** Consider load balancing and scaling strategies to accommodate a growing number of players. Distribute server load across multiple instances or servers if necessary.

Sample WebSocket Code (Client-Side)

Here's a simplified example of establishing a WebSocket connection on the client side using JavaScript and Socket.IO:

```
// Include Socket.IO library

const socket = io();

// Event handler for when the WebSocket connection is established

socket.on('connect', () => {

console.log('Connected to server');

// Send a message to the server

socket.emit('joinGame', { playerName: 'Player 1' });

});
```

Sample WebSocket Code (Server-Side)

On the server side (using Node.js and Socket.IO), you can handle incoming WebSocket messages and broadcast updates to all clients:

```
const io = require('socket.io')(server); // Initialize Socket.IO on your HTTP server

io.on('connection', (socket) => {

console.log('Client connected:', socket.id);
```

```
// Handle incoming messages from clients
socket.on('playerMove', (data) => {
// Process player movement logic and update game state
// Broadcast the updated game state to all connected clients
io.emit('gameStateUpdate', updatedGameState);
});
// Handle player disconnection
socket.on('disconnect', () => {
console.log('Client disconnected:', socket.id);
// Remove the player from the game state and notify other clients
});
});
```

Building a multiplayer environment in Three.js requires a combination of 3D rendering, real-time communication with WebSockets, and server-side logic. With proper synchronization and careful consideration of game mechanics, you can create engaging and immersive multiplayer experiences in web-based 3D applications.

15.3 Synchronizing State Across Clients

One of the critical challenges in building multiplayer 3D environments using Three.js and WebSockets is maintaining synchronized game states across all connected clients. Synchronizing state ensures that all players see the same world, objects, and events, creating a consistent and fair experience. In this section, we'll explore strategies and techniques for achieving state synchronization in multiplayer Three.js applications.

The Importance of State Synchronization

In a multiplayer 3D environment, maintaining synchronized state is essential for several reasons:

1. **Fair Gameplay:** All players should have access to the same game world and information to ensure fairness. Inconsistent states could lead to an unfair advantage for some players.
2. **Realism:** To create an immersive and realistic experience, players should observe the same events and interactions in the shared environment.
3. **Consistency:** Ensuring synchronized state prevents discrepancies and confusion among players. It ensures that actions taken by one player have the expected effects on others.
4. **Interactivity:** Multiplayer environments often involve collaborative or competitive gameplay, requiring precise synchronization of actions and events.

Strategies for State Synchronization

Achieving state synchronization in multiplayer Three.js applications involves several strategies:

1. **Server as Source of Truth:** The server should be the authoritative source of truth for the game state. Clients send their actions and inputs to the server, which processes them, updates the game state, and broadcasts the updated state to all clients.

2. **Player Actions:** Players' actions and inputs (e.g., movement, interactions) should be transmitted to the server in real time. The server then processes these actions and updates the game state accordingly.
3. **Broadcast Updates:** The server should periodically broadcast the game state updates to all connected clients. These updates may include player positions, object positions, events, and other relevant data.
4. **Interpolation and Extrapolation:** To smooth out movement and prevent jitter, clients can use interpolation to estimate object positions between received updates. Additionally, extrapolation can help predict object positions ahead of the server updates, reducing perceived latency.
5. **Delta Compression:** Transmitting only the differences (delta) between the previous and current game states can reduce bandwidth usage. This is especially important for large-scale multiplayer games with many players and objects.
6. **Latency Compensation:** Compensate for network latency by predicting the consequences of player actions on the client side and then adjusting the predictions based on server updates.

Sample Code for State Synchronization

Here's a simplified example of how state synchronization can be implemented in a multiplayer Three.js game using Socket.IO:

```
// Client-side code

const socket = io();

// Handle server updates
```

```
socket.on('gameStateUpdate', (newState) => {
// Interpolate/extrapolate object positions
// Update the client's local game state with the new data
updateGameState(newState);
});
// Send player actions to the server
function sendPlayerAction(action) {
socket.emit('playerAction', action);
}
// Server-side code
const io = require('socket.io')(server);
io.on('connection', (socket) => {
// Handle incoming player actions
socket.on('playerAction', (action) => {
// Process the action and update the game state
const newState = processPlayerAction(action);
// Broadcast the updated game state to all clients
io.emit('gameStateUpdate', newState);
});
});
```

In this example, client and server code demonstrates the transmission of player actions and the synchronization of game state updates. Interpolation and extrapolation techniques can be applied on the client side to provide smooth visual transitions between updates received from the server.

Achieving state synchronization in multiplayer Three.js applications requires careful consideration of network latency, bandwidth optimization, and maintaining a consistent and fair experience for all players. By following best practices and leveraging real-time communication with WebSockets, you can create engaging and immersive multiplayer 3D environments.

15.4 Security Considerations in Networked Applications

Building networked multiplayer 3D applications using Three.js and WebSockets introduces various security considerations. To ensure a safe and secure experience for players, developers must address potential vulnerabilities and implement security measures. In this section, we'll explore key security considerations and strategies for networked applications.

Common Security Concerns

1. **Cheating and Hacking:** In multiplayer games, players may attempt to cheat by manipulating game data or exploiting vulnerabilities. Cheating can ruin the experience for others and compromise game integrity.
2. **Unauthorized Access:** Unauthorized access to game servers or client devices can lead to data breaches, unauthorized actions, and potentially harmful activities.
3. **Data Privacy:** Multiplayer games often involve player

profiles and personal data. Developers must protect this sensitive information and comply with data privacy regulations.

4. **Denial of Service (DoS) Attacks:** Malicious actors may attempt to disrupt game servers by overwhelming them with traffic, causing downtime or lag.

Security Measures

To mitigate these security concerns, consider implementing the following security measures:

1. **Server-Side Validation:** Perform server-side validation of player actions and inputs to prevent cheating. Do not rely solely on client-side validation, as it can be manipulated.
2. **Rate Limiting:** Implement rate limiting to restrict the frequency of actions a player can perform within a certain timeframe. This helps prevent spamming and abuse.
3. **Authentication and Authorization:** Use robust authentication mechanisms to verify the identity of players. Implement authorization checks to ensure that players can only access data and perform actions they are authorized for.
4. **Data Encryption:** Encrypt data transmitted between clients and servers using secure protocols like HTTPS for web applications and WSS (WebSocket Secure) for WebSocket connections.
5. **Secure Password Handling:** If your application requires user accounts, store passwords securely using industry-standard hashing and salting techniques. Avoid storing plaintext passwords.
6. **Access Controls:** Implement access controls to restrict access to sensitive server resources. Ensure that only

authorized users can modify or access certain data.

7. **Monitoring and Logging:** Implement logging and monitoring to detect and respond to security incidents in real time. Track unusual activity patterns and investigate any suspicious behavior.
8. **DoS Protection:** Use DoS protection mechanisms, such as rate limiting and traffic filtering, to mitigate the impact of DoS attacks.
9. **Regular Updates:** Keep server software and libraries up to date to patch known security vulnerabilities. Regularly review and update security policies and procedures.

Code Sample for Server-Side Validation

Here's a simplified example of server-side validation in a multiplayer Three.js game using Node.js and Socket.IO:

```
// Server-side code

const io = require('socket.io')(server);

io.on('connection', (socket) => {

socket.on('playerAction', (action) => {

// Validate player action on the server

if (isValidAction(action)) {

// Process the action and update the game state

const newState = processPlayerAction(action);

// Broadcast the updated game state to all clients

io.emit('gameStateUpdate', newState);
```

```
} else {
// Invalid action, possibly cheating attempt
console.log('Invalid action received from', socket.id);
}
});
});
```

In this example, the server performs server-side validation of player actions by checking if they are valid before processing them. Invalid actions are rejected, preventing potential cheating attempts.

Security is a critical aspect of networked multiplayer 3D applications. By following best practices, staying informed about security threats, and continuously monitoring and updating security measures, developers can create secure and enjoyable multiplayer experiences for players while safeguarding data and gameplay integrity.

15.5 Case Studies: Successful Multiplayer Implementations

To gain a deeper understanding of multiplayer implementations in Three.js and WebSockets, let's explore a few case studies of successful multiplayer 3D applications. These examples demonstrate how real-world projects have leveraged networked multiplayer features to create engaging and interactive experiences.

Case Study 1: "MazeQuest"

"MazeQuest" is a multiplayer maze-solving game built using Three.js and WebSockets. In this game, players navigate through a complex maze filled with challenges and puzzles. The multiplayer aspect allows multiple players to explore the maze together in real time.

Key Features:

- Real-time multiplayer gameplay: Players can see and interact with each other as they navigate the maze.
- Collaborative gameplay: Solving puzzles and challenges often requires teamwork and coordination among players.
- Dynamic level design: The maze is procedurally generated, ensuring a unique experience in each playthrough.

Technical Highlights:

- Server-based maze generation: The server generates the maze and synchronizes it across all clients.
- WebSocket communication: WebSockets are used to transmit player positions, actions, and game state updates.
- Anti-cheat mechanisms: Server-side validation prevents cheating and ensures fair gameplay.

Case Study 2: "SpaceWar VR"

"SpaceWar VR" is a virtual reality (VR) space combat game that allows players to pilot spacecraft in a vast, multiplayer space environment. The game is built using Three.js and WebVR/WebXR for VR support.

Key Features:

- Realistic space combat: Players engage in dogfights and battles in a realistic 3D space environment.

- VR support: Players can immerse themselves in the game using VR headsets.

- Multiplayer battles: The game supports large-scale space battles with multiple players.

Technical Highlights:

- WebVR/WebXR integration: The game leverages WebVR/WebXR APIs to provide VR support directly in the browser.

- WebSocket communication: Real-time communication between players and the server is achieved through WebSockets.

- Server load balancing: To handle a large number of players in space battles, load balancing techniques distribute the load across multiple servers.

Case Study 3: "Dungeon Crawler RPG"

A "Dungeon Crawler RPG" is an isometric multiplayer role-playing game (RPG) built with Three.js. Players explore dungeons, battle monsters, and complete quests in a fantasy world.

Key Features:

- Isometric view: The game features an isometric perspective that adds depth and dimension to the 3D environment.

- Cooperative gameplay: Players can form parties and embark on quests together.

- Quest and story system: The game includes a rich narrative with quests, dialogues, and character progression.

Technical Highlights:

- Custom networking protocol: The game uses a custom WebSocket-based protocol optimized for real-time communication.

- Server-side game logic: The server handles quest progression, enemy AI, and event triggers, ensuring consistent experiences for all players.

- State persistence: Player progress, inventory, and quest status are stored on the server to prevent cheating and data loss.

These case studies illustrate the versatility of Three.js and WebSockets in creating diverse multiplayer 3D experiences, from maze-solving games and space combat simulations to immersive VR experiences and RPGs. Each project showcases the use of real-time communication, synchronization, and collaborative gameplay to engage players in interactive multiplayer environments.

Chapter 16: Advanced Shaders and WebGL

16.1 Deep Dive into GLSL Shaders

In this section, we will take a deep dive into GLSL (OpenGL Shading Language) shaders, which play a crucial role in achieving advanced visual effects in Three.js. Shaders are programs executed by the GPU (Graphics Processing Unit) that control the rendering pipeline and enable developers to create custom rendering effects. To work effectively with shaders in Three.js, it's essential to understand the basics of GLSL and how to integrate shaders into your Three.js projects.

What is GLSL?

GLSL is a C-like language specifically designed for writing shaders. Shaders are used to manipulate the appearance of 3D objects and determine how they react to lighting and other rendering techniques. In Three.js, shaders are written in GLSL and can be attached to materials, allowing you to customize the rendering of objects in your scene.

Shader Types

There are two main types of shaders in Three.js:

1. **Vertex Shaders**: These shaders are responsible for transforming the vertices of 3D models. They execute once for each vertex in a geometry, making them suitable for position calculations.
2. **Fragment Shaders**: Also known as pixel shaders, fragment shaders determine the color of each pixel on the screen.

They execute once for each pixel covered by a 3D object, allowing for detailed color and lighting computations.

Shader Components

A typical GLSL shader consists of several components:

- **Variables**: You can declare variables to store values like positions, colors, and textures.

- **Functions**: Functions allow you to encapsulate complex calculations and reuse code.

- **Main Function**: The main() function is the entry point of a shader. It runs for each vertex (in vertex shaders) or pixel (in fragment shaders).

Uniforms and Attributes

In Three.js, you'll often work with two types of variables in shaders: uniforms and attributes.

- **Uniforms**: Uniforms are values passed from your JavaScript code to the shader. They can be used for things like passing textures, colors, or transformation matrices.

- **Attributes**: Attributes are values associated with each vertex in a geometry. They are used for per-vertex data, like positions or normals.

Example Shader

Here's a simple example of a vertex shader that applies a basic transformation to the vertices of a 3D object:

```
// Vertex Shader

uniform mat4 modelViewMatrix;

uniform mat4 projectionMatrix;

attribute vec3 position;

void main() {

gl_Position = projectionMatrix * modelViewMatrix * vec4(position, 1.0);

}
```

This shader takes the input position of each vertex, transforms it using the model-view and projection matrices, and assigns the final position to gl_Position.

Understanding GLSL shaders is essential for creating custom materials, implementing post-processing effects, and achieving advanced visual effects in your Three.js projects. In the following sections, we'll explore custom shader development, optimization, and integration with Three.js objects.

16.2 Custom Shader Development

Custom shader development in Three.js allows you to unleash your creativity and achieve unique visual effects in your 3D scenes. In this section, we'll explore the process of creating custom shaders, understanding shader components, and integrating them into your Three.js projects.

Shader Structure

A typical shader consists of several parts, including variables, functions, and the main execution function. When developing custom shaders, it's important to understand their structure:

- **Variables**: You can declare various types of variables in shaders, such as float, vec2, vec3, vec4, mat3, and mat4, to hold data like positions, colors, textures, and matrices.

- **Functions**: Functions in shaders allow you to encapsulate complex calculations and promote code reuse. You can define both built-in and custom functions.

- **Main Function**: The main() function serves as the entry point of a shader. It runs for each vertex (in vertex shaders) or pixel (in fragment shaders) and is responsible for generating the final output, such as the position, color, or texture coordinates.

Vertex Shaders

Vertex shaders are responsible for transforming the vertices of 3D models. They execute once for each vertex in a geometry, making them suitable for position calculations, deformations, and other per-vertex operations.

Here's a basic example of a custom vertex shader that applies a simple deformation to a 3D model:

```
// Custom Vertex Shader

uniform float time; // A uniform to control the animation over time

attribute vec3 position; // Input vertex position
```

```
varying vec3 vPosition; // Pass data to the fragment shader

void main() {

// Apply a sine wave deformation to the vertices

float displacement = sin(position.x * 5.0 + time) * 0.1;

vec3 displacedPosition = position + vec3(0.0, displacement, 0.0);

vPosition = displacedPosition; // Pass the modified position to the fragment shader

gl_Position = projectionMatrix * modelViewMatrix * vec4(displacedPosition, 1.0);

}
```

In this example, we deform the vertices based on a sine wave over time. The modified position is passed to the fragment shader through the vPosition variable.

Fragment Shaders

Fragment shaders, also known as pixel shaders, determine the color of each pixel on the screen. They execute once for each pixel covered by a 3D object, allowing for detailed color and lighting computations.

Here's a basic example of a custom fragment shader that applies a color gradient based on the position of each pixel:

```
// Custom Fragment Shader

varying vec3 vPosition; // Input data from the vertex shader

void main() {
```

```
// Create a gradient color based on the Y-coordinate of the pixel position

vec3 color = vec3(0.0, vPosition.y * 0.5 + 0.5, 0.0);

gl_FragColor = vec4(color, 1.0); // Set the final pixel color

}
```

In this example, we use the vPosition variable passed from the vertex shader to create a gradient color effect based on the Y-coordinate of each pixel's position.

Integration in Three.js

To integrate custom shaders into your Three.js project, you'll typically create a new material and attach your shaders to it. Then, you can assign this material to a 3D object. Custom shaders open up possibilities for advanced visual effects, post-processing, and unique rendering techniques in your Three.js scenes.

In the following sections, we'll explore shader optimization, performance considerations, and how to apply shaders to specific objects or scenes in Three.js.

16.3 Optimizing Shader Performance

Optimizing the performance of custom shaders in Three.js is crucial to ensure that your 3D scenes run smoothly and efficiently. In this section, we'll explore various techniques and best practices for optimizing shader performance.

Reduce Redundant Calculations

One of the fundamental principles of shader optimization is to minimize redundant calculations. Shaders often perform complex mathematical operations, and unnecessary calculations can significantly impact performance. To reduce redundancy, consider the following:

- Store intermediate results in variables to reuse them when needed.

- Use conditional statements sparingly, as they can introduce branching and reduce parallelism in shader execution.

Minimize Texture Reads

Texture reads can be expensive in shaders, especially if you're sampling multiple textures. To optimize texture access:

- Combine multiple textures into a single texture atlas to reduce the number of texture reads.

- Use mipmapping and anisotropic filtering when appropriate to improve texture sampling performance.

Avoid Costly Functions

Some GLSL functions can be computationally expensive. Avoid using functions like pow(), exp(), and log() in performance-critical sections of your shader code. Consider alternative approaches or approximations if you need similar functionality.

Use Shader Minification

Shader minification tools can help reduce the size of your shader code by removing whitespace and unnecessary characters. Smaller shader files can load faster and improve runtime performance.

Utilize Shader Preambles

Shader preambles are reusable code segments that you can include at the beginning of multiple shader files. They are useful for defining common functions, constants, or utility code that can be shared across shaders. By centralizing code in preambles, you avoid duplicating code and simplify maintenance.

Limit Iterations

Loops in shaders can be costly, especially if the loop count is dynamic or too large. Whenever possible, try to limit the number of iterations in loops or find alternative approaches that achieve the same result without looping.

Optimize for Mobile and Low-End Devices

If your Three.js application targets mobile devices or low-end hardware, shader optimization becomes even more critical. Test your shaders on a range of devices to ensure they perform well on less powerful GPUs. Consider providing lower-quality shader options for such devices to maintain a smooth user experience.

Profile and Benchmark

Profiling and benchmarking tools can help identify performance bottlenecks in your shaders. Use tools like WebGL Inspector or Chrome DevTools to analyze shader execution times and pinpoint areas that need optimization. Regular profiling can lead to significant performance improvements.

LOD (Level of Detail)

Implementing Level of Detail (LOD) techniques in shaders can be beneficial for objects that are at varying distances from the camera.

LOD allows you to reduce the complexity of the rendering calculations for objects that are far away, improving overall performance.

Caching Uniform Locations

When working with uniforms, consider caching their locations in your shader program to avoid repeated queries. Repeatedly querying uniform locations can be costly. Cache the locations during initialization and update the uniform values as needed.

By following these optimization techniques and continuously testing and profiling your shaders, you can ensure that your custom shaders in Three.js deliver the desired visual effects while maintaining optimal performance in your 3D web applications. Remember that shader optimization is an iterative process, and small adjustments can have a significant impact on performance.

16.4 Visual Effects with Shaders

Custom shaders in Three.js provide a powerful tool for creating a wide range of visual effects in your 3D scenes. In this section, we'll explore some common visual effects that you can achieve through shader programming.

Post-Processing Effects

Post-processing effects are applied to the final rendered image before it is displayed on the screen. They can enhance the visual quality of your scenes or create unique artistic styles. Here are a few examples of post-processing effects:

- **Bloom**: Bloom adds a soft glow to bright areas in the scene, creating a dreamy or cinematic look.

- **Depth of Field**: Depth of field blurs objects that are not in focus, simulating a camera's focus effect.

- **Motion Blur**: Motion blur blurs objects based on their motion, adding realism to fast-moving scenes.

To implement post-processing effects in Three.js, you can use shader passes and render targets. Each effect is typically implemented as a separate shader pass that is applied sequentially to the scene's render output.

Distortion and Warping

Shaders can be used to create distortion and warping effects, such as ripples on water surfaces, heat distortion, or warping for surreal visuals. These effects often involve manipulating vertex positions or fragment coordinates in the shader.

Here's a simple example of a shader that creates a heat distortion effect:

```
// Heat Distortion Shader

uniform sampler2D tDiffuse; // Input texture

uniform float time; // Time uniform for animation

void main() {

// Create a distortion offset based on the pixel's position and time

vec2 distortion = vec2(sin(gl_FragCoord.y * 0.1), cos(gl_FragCoord.x * 0.1 + time * 2.0)) * 0.02;

// Sample the input texture with the distortion offset
```

```
vec4 color = texture2D(tDiffuse, gl_FragCoord.xy / resolution.xy + distortion);

gl_FragColor = color;

}
```

In this shader, we use the time uniform to animate the distortion over time, creating a heat-like effect.

Non-Photorealistic Rendering (NPR)

Non-Photorealistic Rendering techniques aim to create artistic or stylized visuals that deviate from traditional photorealistic rendering. NPR shaders can be used to achieve effects like cel shading, toon shading, or crosshatching.

Here's a simplified example of a toon shading shader:

```
// Toon Shading Shader

varying vec3 vNormal;

void main() {

// Calculate the dot product between the vertex normal and light direction

float lightIntensity = dot(vNormal, normalize(vec3(-1.0, -1.0, -1.0)));

// Apply a threshold to create discrete shading levels

float threshold = 0.3;

if (lightIntensity > threshold) {

gl_FragColor = vec4(1.0, 1.0, 0.0, 1.0); // Yellow
```

```
} else {
gl_FragColor = vec4(0.0, 0.0, 0.0, 1.0); // Black
}
}
```

This shader creates a toon shading effect by quantizing shading levels based on the dot product between the vertex normal and the light direction.

Advanced Visual Effects

Advanced visual effects, such as realistic water simulations, particle systems, or complex lighting models, often require intricate shaders and techniques. These effects leverage the full power of shader programming to deliver stunning visuals in Three.js.

For example, simulating water can involve a combination of reflection, refraction, wave simulation, and foam generation shaders. Similarly, particle systems can use shaders to control particle motion, size, and color based on various factors like wind and collision.

The possibilities for visual effects with shaders in Three.js are virtually limitless, and they allow you to push the boundaries of realism and creativity in your 3D web applications. By experimenting with custom shaders, you can craft unique and visually captivating experiences for your users.

16.5 Integrating Shaders with Three.js Objects

Integrating custom shaders with Three.js objects allows you to apply unique visual effects to specific parts of your 3D scene. In this section, we'll explore how to attach shaders to objects, work with shader materials, and achieve fine-grained control over shader application.

Shader Materials

In Three.js, shader materials are used to associate shaders with specific objects in your scene. You can create a custom shader material by extending the THREE.ShaderMaterial class and specifying your custom vertex and fragment shaders.

Here's a basic example of creating a custom shader material and attaching it to a mesh:

```
// Define custom vertex and fragment shaders as strings

const vertexShader = `

// Your custom vertex shader code here

`;

const fragmentShader = `

// Your custom fragment shader code here

`;

// Create a ShaderMaterial

const shaderMaterial = new THREE.ShaderMaterial({

vertexShader: vertexShader,

fragmentShader: fragmentShader,

});
```

```
// Create a mesh and assign the shader material

const geometry = new THREE.BoxGeometry(1, 1, 1);

const mesh = new THREE.Mesh(geometry, shaderMaterial);

// Add the mesh to the scene

scene.add(mesh);
```

By using shader materials, you can apply custom shaders to objects like meshes, particles, or lines, giving you fine-grained control over their appearance.

Uniforms and Attributes

Shader materials allow you to pass data to shaders using uniforms and attributes:

- **Uniforms**: Uniforms are values that you can set from your JavaScript code and access in your shaders. They are used for passing things like textures, colors, matrices, and time values.

- **Attributes**: Attributes are values associated with each vertex in a geometry. They can be used for per-vertex data like positions, normals, or custom attributes.

To work with uniforms and attributes, you'll need to declare them in your shader code and set their values in your JavaScript code.

Applying Shaders to Specific Objects

You can apply shaders to specific objects or groups of objects in your scene. This allows you to have different visual effects for different parts of your 3D scene. Here's an example of how to apply a custom shader to a specific mesh:

```
// Assuming you have a mesh named 'myMesh' and a shader material named 'myShaderMaterial'

// Assign the shader material to the mesh

myMesh.material = myShaderMaterial;
```

You can also apply shaders to groups of objects or use them conditionally based on user interactions, object proximity, or other factors.

Shader Passes and Post-Processing

Shader passes are used for post-processing effects, allowing you to apply shaders to the final rendered image before it's displayed on the screen. To create post-processing effects, you can use libraries like three.js's EffectComposer and ShaderPass.

Here's a simplified example of applying a post-processing shader pass:

```
// Create an EffectComposer

const composer = new THREE.EffectComposer(renderer);

// Create a RenderPass

const renderPass = new THREE.RenderPass(scene, camera);

composer.addPass(renderPass);

// Create a custom shader pass

const customPass = new THREE.ShaderPass(customShader);
```

```
composer.addPass(customPass);

// Render the composer instead of the default renderer

composer.render();
```

By using shader passes, you can apply a wide range of post-processing effects to your entire scene.

Dynamic Shader Updates

In some cases, you may need to dynamically update shader code during runtime, for example, to respond to user interactions or changing scene conditions. To do this, you can update the vertexShader and fragmentShader properties of your shader material and then call material.needsUpdate = true to inform Three.js that the shaders need recompilation.

```
// Update shader code dynamically

shaderMaterial.vertexShader = updatedVertexShader;

shaderMaterial.fragmentShader = updatedFragmentShader;

// Inform Three.js that shaders need recompilation

shaderMaterial.needsUpdate = true;
```

This allows you to create interactive and dynamic shader effects in your Three.js applications.

Integrating custom shaders with Three.js objects opens up a world of possibilities for creating unique and visually captivating 3D web experiences. Whether you want to apply shaders to specific objects or implement post-processing effects, understanding how to work with shader materials and passes gives you the tools to craft stunning visuals in your projects.

Chapter 17: Mobile Development with Three.js

17.1 Adapting Three.js for Mobile Devices

Mobile devices have become an integral part of our daily lives, and delivering immersive 3D experiences on smartphones and tablets is essential. In this section, we'll explore how to adapt Three.js for mobile development, addressing various considerations and best practices.

Responsive Design

The first step in mobile development with Three.js is ensuring your 3D web application is responsive. Responsive design means that your application adapts to different screen sizes and orientations. To achieve this:

- Use relative units (e.g., percentages) for layout elements to accommodate varying screen dimensions.
- Implement media queries in your CSS to adjust styles based on screen width and orientation.
- Consider touch-friendly controls and user interfaces suitable for touchscreens.

Performance Optimization

Mobile devices typically have less processing power and memory than desktop computers, making performance optimization crucial:

- **Simplify Geometry**: Reduce the complexity of 3D models and scenes to minimize the rendering load.

- **Texture Compression**: Use texture compression formats like ETC2 or PVRTC for efficient texture rendering on mobile GPUs.

- **Level of Detail (LOD)**: Implement LOD techniques to reduce the level of detail for objects that are far from the camera.

- **Mobile-First Shaders**: Optimize shaders for mobile GPUs, considering their limitations.

Touch Interfaces and Gestures

Mobile devices rely on touch interfaces, so you'll need to implement touch and gesture controls in your Three.js application:

- Use libraries like Hammer.js to handle touch gestures like tapping, swiping, and pinching.

- Implement touch-based camera controls for navigation within the 3D scene, allowing users to pan, zoom, and rotate.

- Ensure that touch interactions are intuitive and responsive to provide a smooth user experience.

Performance Testing

Testing your mobile application on a variety of devices is essential to identify performance bottlenecks and ensure compatibility:

- Use device simulators/emulators or physical devices to test your application on different Android and iOS devices.

- Monitor performance metrics like frame rate, memory usage, and CPU/GPU load to identify areas that need improvement.

- Address any issues specific to certain devices or browsers, and consider fallback options for less capable devices.

Mobile VR and AR Considerations

If your application includes Virtual Reality (VR) or Augmented Reality (AR) features, consider the following:

- Ensure compatibility with mobile VR headsets like Google Cardboard, Daydream, or Oculus Quest.

- Implement AR experiences that use the device's camera and sensors, considering factors like tracking quality and performance.

- Optimize rendering for stereoscopic displays in VR to maintain a high frame rate.

Progressive Web App (PWA)

Consider turning your Three.js application into a Progressive Web App (PWA) to improve accessibility and user engagement:

- PWAs can be installed on a user's home screen, providing a native-like experience without the need to download from an app store.

• Implement service workers to enable offline functionality and faster loading times.

• Ensure your PWA is responsive and performs well on both mobile and desktop.

Mobile-First Design

Adopting a mobile-first design approach ensures that your application's core functionality works seamlessly on mobile devices before scaling up to larger screens. This approach aligns with modern development practices and user expectations.

By following these best practices and considerations, you can adapt Three.js for mobile development and create 3D web applications that provide a smooth and engaging experience on smartphones and tablets.

17.2 Touch Interfaces and Gestures

Implementing touch interfaces and gestures in your Three.js application is essential for providing a user-friendly experience on mobile devices. Touch controls allow users to interact with 3D scenes using their fingers, making navigation and interaction more intuitive. In this section, we'll explore how to integrate touch interfaces and gestures into your mobile Three.js application.

Touch Events

To capture touch interactions in your Three.js application, you can use the standard touch events provided by web browsers. These events include:

• touchstart: Triggered when a user touches the screen.

- touchmove: Fired as the user's finger moves across the screen.
- touchend: Occurs when the user lifts their finger off the screen.
- touchcancel: Fired if the touch event is canceled for any reason.

You can add event listeners to your HTML elements or directly to your Three.js canvas to capture these touch events.

```
// Adding a touch event listener to the Three.js canvas

const canvas = document.getElementById('your-canvas-id');

canvas.addEventListener('touchstart', onTouchStart, false);

canvas.addEventListener('touchmove', onTouchMove, false);

canvas.addEventListener('touchend', onTouchEnd, false);

function onTouchStart(event) {

// Handle touchstart event

}

function onTouchMove(event) {

// Handle touchmove event

}

function onTouchEnd(event) {

// Handle touchend event

}
```

Touch Gestures

Handling touch gestures often involves more complex interactions, such as pinch-to-zoom, two-finger rotation, or swiping. Libraries like Hammer.js make it easier to work with touch gestures in your Three.js application.

Here's a basic example of using Hammer.js to implement pinch-to-zoom and pan gestures:

```
// Import Hammer.js library

import Hammer from 'hammerjs';

// Create a Hammer.js instance for your canvas

const canvas = document.getElementById('your-canvas-id');

const hammer = new Hammer(canvas);

// Enable pinch-to-zoom and panning gestures

hammer.get('pinch').set({ enable: true });

hammer.get('pan').set({ direction: Hammer.DIRECTION_ALL });

// Add gesture event listeners

hammer.on('pinch', onPinch);

hammer.on('pan', onPan);

function onPinch(event) {

// Handle pinch-to-zoom gesture

const scale = event.scale;

// Adjust camera or object scale based on the pinch scale value
```

```
}

function onPan(event) {

// Handle panning gesture

const deltaX = event.deltaX;

const deltaY = event.deltaY;

// Translate camera or object based on deltaX and deltaY

}
```

By using Hammer.js or similar libraries, you can implement a wide range of touch gestures in your Three.js application, enhancing user interactivity.

Virtual Joysticks and Buttons

For games and interactive experiences, you may need on-screen virtual joysticks, buttons, or other touch controls. These elements can be implemented using HTML and CSS and integrated with your Three.js application.

Here's a simple example of an HTML-based virtual joystick:

```
<div id="joystick">

<div id="joystick-stick"></div>

</div>
```

You can then use JavaScript to capture touch events on the joystick element and control your 3D scene accordingly.

```
const joystick = document.getElementById('joystick');
```

```
const joystickStick = document.getElementById('joystick-stick');
joystick.addEventListener('touchstart', onTouchStart);
joystick.addEventListener('touchmove', onTouchMove);
joystick.addEventListener('touchend', onTouchEnd);
function onTouchStart(event) {
// Handle joystick touchstart
}
function onTouchMove(event) {
// Handle joystick touchmove
// Calculate the position of the joystick stick
}
function onTouchEnd(event) {
// Handle joystick touchend
}
```

By combining HTML-based touch controls with your Three.js application, you can create immersive and interactive mobile experiences that are well-suited for gaming and other applications.

Testing and Optimization

When implementing touch interfaces and gestures, it's essential to thoroughly test your application on various mobile devices and browsers to ensure compatibility. Pay attention to performance, responsiveness, and the overall user experience. Consider optimizing touch interactions for smaller screens and ensuring that gestures work smoothly across different devices.

By integrating touch interfaces and gestures effectively into your Three.js application, you can provide an engaging and intuitive experience for mobile users, making your 3D content accessible on smartphones and tablets.

17.3 Performance Optimization for Mobile

Optimizing the performance of your Three.js application for mobile devices is crucial to ensure a smooth and enjoyable user experience. Mobile devices often have limited processing power and memory compared to desktop computers, so it's essential to follow best practices to maximize performance. In this section, we'll explore various techniques for optimizing performance in mobile Three.js applications.

Simplify Geometry

Reducing the complexity of 3D models and scenes can significantly improve performance on mobile devices. Here are some strategies to simplify geometry:

- **Reduce Vertex Count**: Use lower-poly models or apply level-of-detail techniques to decrease the number of vertices in your 3D objects.

- **Merge Geometries**: Combine multiple objects with similar materials into a single geometry to minimize draw calls.

- **Use Instancing**: Implement instanced rendering for objects that share the same geometry and material but have different transformations.

Texture Compression

Efficient texture usage is critical for mobile performance. Consider the following texture optimization techniques:

- **Texture Atlases**: Combine multiple textures into a single texture atlas to reduce the number of texture switches and improve batching.

- **Texture Compression Formats**: Use texture compression formats like ETC2 or PVRTC for mobile GPUs to reduce memory and bandwidth usage.

- **Texture Size**: Keep textures as small as possible while maintaining acceptable quality. Avoid oversized textures that consume unnecessary memory.

Level of Detail (LOD)

Implementing Level of Detail (LOD) techniques is essential for optimizing performance on mobile devices. LOD involves using simplified versions of 3D models when they are far from the camera, reducing rendering complexity. Three.js provides built-in support for LOD.

Mobile-Friendly Shaders

Mobile GPUs have different capabilities and limitations compared to desktop GPUs. To optimize shader performance for mobile:

- Avoid using expensive shader functions and calculations.
- Test and profile shaders on actual mobile devices to ensure they run smoothly.
- Use simpler shaders for objects that are less visually significant.

Occlusion Culling

Implementing occlusion culling can prevent rendering objects that are not visible to the camera, saving valuable GPU resources. Three.js has tools and libraries that can help you achieve occlusion culling in your mobile application.

Reduce Draw Calls

Minimizing the number of draw calls is critical for mobile performance. Strategies to reduce draw calls include:

- Batch objects with the same materials and geometries to reduce draw calls.
- Use hardware instancing when applicable to render multiple instances of the same object efficiently.
- Implement techniques like mesh merging for objects with similar characteristics.

Mobile-Optimized Lighting

Lighting can have a significant impact on performance. Optimize lighting in your mobile Three.js application by:

- Using simpler lighting models when possible.
- Reducing the number of active lights in the scene.
- Applying baked lighting for static scenes to avoid expensive real-time calculations.

Testing and Profiling

Thoroughly test your mobile Three.js application on a variety of devices to ensure it performs well. Use performance profiling tools to identify bottlenecks and areas for improvement. Monitor critical metrics like frame rate, memory usage, and CPU/GPU load during testing.

Progressive Loading

Implement progressive loading to load and display assets as needed, reducing initial load times. Prioritize loading essential assets first and load secondary assets in the background during gameplay or navigation.

By applying these performance optimization techniques, you can ensure that your Three.js application runs smoothly on a wide range of mobile devices, providing users with a responsive and enjoyable 3D experience on smartphones and tablets.

17.4 Mobile VR and AR Considerations

Mobile Virtual Reality (VR) and Augmented Reality (AR) have gained significant popularity, and integrating VR and AR features into your Three.js application for mobile devices can provide immersive experiences. In this section, we'll explore considerations and best practices for developing mobile VR and AR applications using Three.js.

VR on Mobile

Mobile VR allows users to experience virtual reality using smartphones and affordable VR headsets like Google Cardboard, Daydream, or Oculus Quest. Here are some key considerations for developing VR applications on mobile devices:

- **Performance**: VR demands a high and consistent frame rate (usually 60 FPS or higher) to avoid motion sickness. Optimize your VR application for performance by simplifying geometry, reducing texture sizes, and using mobile-friendly shaders.

- **Stereoscopic Rendering**: VR requires rendering two slightly different views for each eye to create a 3D effect. Three.js provides built-in support for stereoscopic rendering, so you don't need to handle this manually.

- **Controller Support**: Some VR headsets come with controllers or support external controllers. Ensure your application can handle controller input for interaction and navigation.

- **VR Comfort**: Pay attention to VR comfort. Minimize motion sickness by avoiding rapid camera movements or excessive acceleration in your VR experiences.

- **Orientation and Position Tracking**: Some mobile VR headsets provide orientation and position tracking capabilities. Use Three.js to integrate these features for more immersive VR experiences.

AR on Mobile

Augmented Reality (AR) enhances the real world with virtual elements, often using a device's camera and sensors. Mobile AR applications can be developed using AR frameworks like ARKit (iOS) and ARCore (Android). Here are considerations for AR development with Three.js:

- **Device Compatibility**: Ensure your target devices support AR capabilities and have the necessary sensors and camera.

- **Geolocation**: Use geolocation data to anchor virtual objects in the real world accurately.

- **Camera Integration**: Integrate the device's camera feed into your AR application to blend virtual and real elements seamlessly.

- **Scene Understanding**: Leverage AR frameworks' scene understanding capabilities to detect and interact with real-world objects and surfaces.

- **User Interface**: Design intuitive and non-intrusive user interfaces for AR applications, as users need to see both virtual and real-world content simultaneously.

- **Performance**: Optimize your AR application for performance, as AR can be resource-intensive. Efficient rendering and asset management are crucial.

Cross-Platform Considerations

If you plan to develop VR and AR applications for both Android and iOS, consider cross-platform frameworks like WebXR and

WebAR that leverage web technologies. Three.js has support for WebXR and WebAR, allowing you to create AR and VR experiences that can run on both platforms.

Testing and User Feedback

Extensive testing on a variety of devices is essential when developing mobile VR and AR applications. Ensure that your application works smoothly, provides accurate tracking and rendering, and offers a comfortable user experience. Gather user feedback to identify any issues or improvements needed.

By carefully considering these factors and integrating mobile VR and AR capabilities into your Three.js applications, you can create compelling and immersive experiences that take full advantage of the capabilities offered by modern smartphones and tablets. Whether you're building a VR game or an AR app, Three.js provides the tools and flexibility needed for successful mobile VR and AR development.

17.5 Case Studies in Mobile 3D Applications

In this section, we'll explore some case studies of real-world mobile 3D applications built with Three.js. These examples showcase the versatility of Three.js in creating engaging and interactive experiences on mobile devices.

1. Matterport 3D Showcase:

Matterport[5] is a popular platform for creating and exploring 3D models of real-world spaces. Their mobile application allows users to virtually tour properties, museums, and other locations. Three.js is at the core of their 3D rendering engine, enabling smooth navigation

5. https://matterport.com/

and interaction with 3D environments. Users can explore spaces in virtual reality, making it a valuable tool for real estate and interior design.

2. Sketchfab:

Sketchfab[6] is a community-driven platform for sharing and exploring 3D content. Their mobile app lets users view, upload, and interact with 3D models on smartphones and tablets. Three.js plays a vital role in rendering and displaying the vast library of 3D models available on Sketchfab. Users can explore detailed models, rotate and zoom in, and even view them in AR.

3. Pokémon GO:

Pokémon GO[7] is a mobile AR game that became a global phenomenon. While the game's primary focus is AR, Three.js is used for rendering 3D models during encounters with Pokémon. The combination of AR and 3D graphics creates a seamless and immersive experience where players can see and interact with Pokémon in the real world through their mobile devices.

4. IKEA Place:

IKEA Place[8] is an AR app that allows users to visualize how IKEA furniture would look in their homes. Three.js is used for rendering 3D furniture models in the app. Users can place virtual furniture in their real environment through their device's camera, helping them make informed purchasing decisions.

---

6. https://sketchfab.com/
7. https://www.pokemongo.com/
8. https://www.ikea.com/us/en/planners/ikea-place/

5. Paint Space AR:

Paint Space AR[9] is an AR painting app that lets users create artwork in augmented reality. Three.js is used for rendering brushes, strokes, and 3D objects in the AR space. Users can unleash their creativity by painting in the real world and seeing their creations from different angles on their mobile devices.

6. JW Library:

JW Library[10] is a mobile app developed by Jehovah's Witnesses that includes an extensive library of publications and videos. The app features interactive 3D animations created with Three.js to illustrate Bible stories and concepts. These 3D animations enhance the app's educational content and engage users in a unique way.

These case studies demonstrate the versatility of Three.js in mobile applications across various industries, from real estate and gaming to education and retail. Whether it's rendering 3D models, creating immersive AR experiences, or enhancing user engagement, Three.js empowers developers to deliver rich and interactive 3D content on smartphones and tablets.

9. https://www.paintspacear.com/

10. https://www.jw.org/en/jw-library/

Chapter 18: Artistic and Creative Uses of Three.js

18.1 Three.js in Digital Art

Three.js has found a significant presence in the world of digital art, enabling artists to create interactive and visually stunning pieces that push the boundaries of traditional art forms. Whether it's creating generative art, interactive installations, or immersive exhibitions, Three.js offers a powerful canvas for artistic expression.

Generative Art

Generative art involves using algorithms and rules to create art dynamically. Three.js is well-suited for generative art due to its ability to render complex 3D scenes in real-time. Artists can program their visual and audio creations, producing mesmerizing and ever-evolving artworks.

```
// Example of a simple generative art scene in Three.js

const scene = new THREE.Scene();

const camera = new THREE.PerspectiveCamera(75, window.innerWidth / window.innerHeight, 0.1, 1000);

const renderer = new THREE.WebGLRenderer();

renderer.setSize(window.innerWidth, window.innerHeight);

document.body.appendChild(renderer.domElement);

const geometry = new THREE.TorusKnotGeometry(10, 3, 100, 16);
```

```
const material = new THREE.MeshBasicMaterial({ color: 0xff00ff
});

const torusKnot = new THREE.Mesh(geometry, material);

scene.add(torusKnot);

camera.position.z = 30;

const animate = () => {

requestAnimationFrame(animate);

torusKnot.rotation.x += 0.01;

torusKnot.rotation.y += 0.01;

renderer.render(scene, camera);

};

animate();
```

Interactive Installations and Exhibitions

Three.js has been instrumental in creating interactive art installations and exhibitions. Artists and designers can merge physical and digital elements to engage audiences in unique and immersive experiences. Sensors, cameras, and other input devices can be integrated with Three.js to create responsive and interactive installations.

```
// Example of interactive installation with Three.js and sensors

const scene = new THREE.Scene();

const camera = new THREE.PerspectiveCamera(75,
window.innerWidth / window.innerHeight, 0.1, 1000);
```

```
const renderer = new THREE.WebGLRenderer();
renderer.setSize(window.innerWidth, window.innerHeight);
document.body.appendChild(renderer.domElement);
// Add interactive elements and sensors here
const animate = () => {
requestAnimationFrame(animate);
// Update interactive elements based on sensor input
renderer.render(scene, camera);
};
animate();
```

Bridging Art and Technology

Three.js has become a bridge between traditional art forms and technology-driven art. Artists are increasingly using Three.js to incorporate 3D graphics, animations, and interactivity into their work. This fusion of art and technology has given rise to innovative and boundary-pushing art forms that captivate and inspire audiences.

Creative Coding with Three.js

Creative coders and artists are drawn to Three.js because of its accessibility and flexibility. With a basic understanding of JavaScript and Three.js, artists can experiment and create captivating visuals and interactive experiences. This democratization of 3D graphics and interactive art has opened up new avenues for creative expression.

Community Contributions and Collaborations

The Three.js community has grown exponentially, with artists, developers, and creative enthusiasts coming together to share their knowledge and creations. Open-source projects, libraries, and frameworks built on top of Three.js further empower artists to explore innovative artistic possibilities. Collaboration between artists and developers has resulted in groundbreaking digital art experiences that challenge conventions and inspire future generations of creators.

In this digital age, Three.js has emerged as a powerful tool for artists to push the boundaries of their creativity. From generative art to interactive installations, Three.js empowers artists to create immersive and boundary-breaking digital artworks that redefine the art landscape. As technology continues to evolve, Three.js will undoubtedly remain at the forefront of artistic and creative endeavors, bridging the gap between art and technology.

18.2 Interactive Installations and Exhibitions

Interactive installations and exhibitions have gained prominence in the art world, offering audiences a chance to engage with art in novel and immersive ways. Three.js plays a pivotal role in creating these interactive experiences, where the physical and digital realms merge to captivate and inspire viewers.

Immersive Environments

Three.js allows artists and designers to build immersive environments that respond to user interactions. These environments often use large screens, projectors, or VR headsets to envelop viewers. Whether it's a gallery exhibition or a public installation, Three.js provides the tools to create visually stunning and interactive spaces.

```
// Example of an interactive 3D art installation with Three.js
const scene = new THREE.Scene();
const camera = new THREE.PerspectiveCamera(75, window.innerWidth / window.innerHeight, 0.1, 1000);
const renderer = new THREE.WebGLRenderer();
renderer.setSize(window.innerWidth, window.innerHeight);
document.body.appendChild(renderer.domElement);
// Add 3D models, animations, and interactivity to the scene
const animate = () => {
requestAnimationFrame(animate);
// Update animations and interactions based on user input
renderer.render(scene, camera);
};
animate();
```

Sensors and Input Devices

Interactive installations often incorporate sensors and input devices to detect user actions. These sensors can include motion detectors, touchscreens, cameras, or even custom-built input devices. Three.js can seamlessly integrate with these sensors, allowing artists to create responsive and dynamic experiences.

```
// Example of integrating a motion sensor with Three.js
const motionSensor = new MotionSensor();
```

```
motionSensor.onMotionDetected = () => {

// Trigger animations or interactions based on motion

};

// Example of integrating a touchscreen with Three.js

const touchscreen = new Touchscreen();

touchscreen.onTouchStart = (event) => {

// Handle touch interactions in the Three.js scene

};

// Add more sensors and input devices as needed
```

Real-Time Interaction

One of the strengths of Three.js is its ability to provide real-time interaction. Viewers can actively participate in the art piece, influencing its behavior and appearance. This dynamic engagement fosters a deeper connection between the audience and the artwork.

```
// Example of real-time interaction in a Three.js art installation

const scene = new THREE.Scene();

const camera = new THREE.PerspectiveCamera(75, window.innerWidth / window.innerHeight, 0.1, 1000);

const renderer = new THREE.WebGLRenderer();

renderer.setSize(window.innerWidth, window.innerHeight);

document.body.appendChild(renderer.domElement);

// Add interactive elements and real-time feedback mechanisms
```

```
const animate = () => {
requestAnimationFrame(animate);
// Update interactive elements and respond to user input
renderer.render(scene, camera);
};
animate();
```

Collaborative Experiences

Interactive installations often encourage collaboration among viewers. Multiple users can interact with the art simultaneously, creating a shared experience. Three.js can handle the complexities of coordinating interactions among multiple participants, making collaborative installations a reality.

Accessibility and Inclusivity

Artistic installations aim to be inclusive and accessible to diverse audiences. Three.js allows for accessibility features such as adjustable font sizes, alternative input methods, and audio descriptions. These considerations ensure that interactive art installations are enjoyable and meaningful for everyone.

Testing and User Experience

Extensive testing is crucial to ensure that interactive installations function as intended and provide a seamless user experience. Artists and developers collaborate to refine the interactive elements and address any technical or usability issues that may arise during testing.

Interactive installations and exhibitions powered by Three.js are pushing the boundaries of traditional art forms. These immersive and engaging experiences blur the lines between art and technology, inviting viewers to become active participants in the creative process. As technology continues to evolve, Three.js will remain at the forefront of the interactive art world, enabling artists to conceive and execute innovative and captivating installations.

18.3 Bridging Art and Technology

The fusion of art and technology has given rise to groundbreaking creative expressions, and Three.js has played a pivotal role in bridging these two worlds. Artists are increasingly leveraging the capabilities of Three.js to push the boundaries of traditional art forms, creating innovative and immersive experiences that captivate audiences.

Interactive Sculptures

Three.js enables artists to transform digital models into interactive sculptures. These sculptures can react to user input, such as touch or motion, bringing a dynamic element to traditionally static art forms. Sculptures can change shape, color, or sound in response to viewer interactions, creating engaging and participatory art experiences.

```
// Example of an interactive sculpture with Three.js

const scene = new THREE.Scene();

const camera = new THREE.PerspectiveCamera(75, window.innerWidth / window.innerHeight, 0.1, 1000);

const renderer = new THREE.WebGLRenderer();

renderer.setSize(window.innerWidth, window.innerHeight);
```

```
document.body.appendChild(renderer.domElement);

// Create a 3D sculpture and add interactive elements

const animate = () => {

requestAnimationFrame(animate);

// Update the sculpture's appearance based on user input

renderer.render(scene, camera);

};

animate();
```

Projection Mapping

Projection mapping involves projecting images or animations onto physical surfaces, transforming them into dynamic and interactive canvases. Three.js can be integrated with projection mapping technology to create mesmerizing and immersive installations. Artists can use this technique to manipulate the perception of space and transform ordinary objects into extraordinary art pieces.

```
// Example of projection mapping with Three.js

const projector = new Projector();

projector.loadContent('projected-image.jpg'); // Load the content to be projected

projector.onUserInteraction = () => {

// Adjust the projection based on user input

};
```

// Calibrate the projector and the physical surface for precise mapping

Data-Driven Art

Data-driven art leverages real-time data to create dynamic and ever-changing artworks. Three.js can be used to visualize data in artistic and expressive ways, turning statistics, environmental data, or other information into visually captivating pieces. Data-driven art not only communicates information but also evokes emotions and insights.

```
// Example of data-driven art with Three.js

const scene = new THREE.Scene();

const camera = new THREE.PerspectiveCamera(75, window.innerWidth / window.innerHeight, 0.1, 1000);

const renderer = new THREE.WebGLRenderer();

renderer.setSize(window.innerWidth, window.innerHeight);

document.body.appendChild(renderer.domElement);

// Visualize real-time data in an artistic and meaningful manner

const animate = () => {

requestAnimationFrame(animate);

// Update the visualization with new data

renderer.render(scene, camera);

};

animate();
```

Collaborative Art Projects

Three.js facilitates collaborative art projects where artists and technologists work together to create immersive and interactive artworks. The collaboration often involves artists providing creative direction and vision, while developers implement the technical aspects using Three.js. This partnership results in art that seamlessly integrates creativity and technology.

Experimental Storytelling

Artists use Three.js to experiment with new forms of storytelling. Interactive narratives, virtual worlds, and digital storytelling experiences can be crafted using Three.js. These projects push the boundaries of traditional storytelling, allowing audiences to become active participants in the narrative.

Art and Technology Festivals

Art and technology festivals around the world showcase the synergy between these two domains. Three.js is frequently featured in such festivals, powering installations, exhibitions, and performances that blur the lines between art and technology. These festivals provide a platform for artists to push the boundaries of their creativity.

Three.js continues to serve as a bridge between art and technology, enabling artists to realize their visions and create art that transcends traditional boundaries. The versatile and accessible nature of Three.js empowers artists to experiment, innovate, and captivate audiences with immersive and interactive art experiences. As technology evolves, Three.js will remain a vital tool for artists seeking to explore the limitless possibilities of creative expression.

18.4 Creative Coding with Three.js

Creative coding refers to the practice of writing code to create artworks, animations, and interactive experiences. Three.js provides a versatile platform for creative coders to explore their ideas, experiment with visual concepts, and push the boundaries of digital art. Here, we'll delve into the exciting world of creative coding with Three.js.

Expressive Visuals

Three.js empowers creative coders to generate expressive visuals through code. Artists can manipulate 3D geometries, textures, and materials to create intricate and visually stunning scenes. With the flexibility of JavaScript and Three.js, artists have full control over every aspect of their digital creations.

```
// Example of creating expressive visuals with Three.js

const scene = new THREE.Scene();

const camera = new THREE.PerspectiveCamera(75, window.innerWidth / window.innerHeight, 0.1, 1000);

const renderer = new THREE.WebGLRenderer();

renderer.setSize(window.innerWidth, window.innerHeight);

document.body.appendChild(renderer.domElement);

// Create complex 3D geometries, apply materials, and set up lighting

const animate = () => {

requestAnimationFrame(animate);

// Apply transformations and animations to the 3D scene
```

```
renderer.render(scene, camera);

};

animate();
```

Procedural Generation

Creative coders can utilize procedural generation techniques to generate complex and dynamic content. Whether it's procedurally generated landscapes, fractal art, or abstract animations, Three.js provides the tools to implement these algorithms and bring creative visions to life.

```
// Example of procedural generation with Three.js

const scene = new THREE.Scene();

const camera = new THREE.PerspectiveCamera(75, window.innerWidth / window.innerHeight, 0.1, 1000);

const renderer = new THREE.WebGLRenderer();

renderer.setSize(window.innerWidth, window.innerHeight);

document.body.appendChild(renderer.domElement);

// Implement procedural generation algorithms to create dynamic content

const animate = () => {

requestAnimationFrame(animate);

// Continuously update the procedurally generated content

renderer.render(scene, camera);
```

```
};

animate();
```

Interactive Experiences

Creative coding with Three.js extends to interactive experiences where users can actively engage with digital artworks. Artists can implement user interfaces, gestures, and inputs to enable interaction, turning passive viewers into active participants in the creative process.

```
// Example of interactive experiences with Three.js

const scene = new THREE.Scene();

const camera = new THREE.PerspectiveCamera(75, window.innerWidth / window.innerHeight, 0.1, 1000);

const renderer = new THREE.WebGLRenderer();

renderer.setSize(window.innerWidth, window.innerHeight);

document.body.appendChild(renderer.domElement);

// Create interactive elements and implement user input handling

const animate = () => {

requestAnimationFrame(animate);

// Respond to user input and update the interactive elements

renderer.render(scene, camera);

};

animate();
```

Audio-Visual Synchrony

Creative coders can explore the intersection of sound and visuals using Three.js. By synchronizing audio and visual elements, artists can create immersive audio-visual experiences. This synergy between music and graphics adds another layer of depth to digital artworks.

```
// Example of audio-visual synchrony with Three.js

const scene = new THREE.Scene();

const camera = new THREE.PerspectiveCamera(75, window.innerWidth / window.innerHeight, 0.1, 1000);

const renderer = new THREE.WebGLRenderer();

renderer.setSize(window.innerWidth, window.innerHeight);

document.body.appendChild(renderer.domElement);

// Combine audio elements with visual animations, ensuring synchrony

const animate = () => {

requestAnimationFrame(animate);

// Keep the audio and visual elements in sync

renderer.render(scene, camera);

};

animate();
```

Creative Community

The creative coding community is vibrant and collaborative, with artists and coders sharing their creations, techniques, and ideas.

Open-source libraries and frameworks built on top of Three.js further facilitate creative coding endeavors. Collaboration and knowledge exchange within the community inspire fresh perspectives and innovative approaches to digital art.

Creative coding with Three.js represents a fusion of artistic expression and programming creativity. Whether you're an artist exploring new digital realms or a coder seeking to create visually captivating and interactive experiences, Three.js provides a platform that empowers you to push the boundaries of creative coding and digital art. The possibilities are endless, and the only limit is your imagination.

18.5 Community Contributions and Collaborations

The Three.js community has grown into a vibrant and collaborative ecosystem, bringing together artists, developers, and creative enthusiasts from around the world. This section explores the significance of community contributions and collaborations within the context of Three.js.

Open-Source Culture

At the heart of the Three.js community lies an open-source ethos. Three.js itself is an open-source project, meaning that its source code is freely available for anyone to view, modify, and contribute to. This open-source culture encourages transparency, collaboration, and the democratization of 3D web graphics.

```
// Example of a simple Three.js contribution

function customThreeJsFeature() {
```

```
// Implement a new feature or enhancement
}
// Share the code with the Three.js community through platforms like GitHub
```

Libraries and Frameworks

The community has produced numerous libraries and frameworks built on top of Three.js, extending its capabilities and simplifying complex tasks. These contributions cover areas such as physics simulations, animation tools, shader libraries, and more. These libraries serve as invaluable resources for both beginners and experienced developers.

```
// Example of using a community-built Three.js library
import { PhysicsLoader } from 'three.physics';
import { AnimationFramework } from 'my-threejs-animations';
const physics = new PhysicsLoader();
const animations = new AnimationFramework();
```

Tutorials and Documentation

Contributors within the community create tutorials and documentation to help newcomers learn and master Three.js. These resources range from beginner-friendly introductions to in-depth guides on advanced topics. They play a crucial role in reducing the learning curve and enabling aspiring developers and artists to get started with Three.js.

- [Getting Started with Three.js]*(https://example.com/getting-started)*

- [Advanced Three.js Animation Techniques]*(https://example.com/advanced-animation)*

- [Creating Realistic Materials in Three.js]*(https://example.com/realistic-materials)*

Collaboration Platforms

Collaboration platforms such as GitHub provide a space for community members to collaborate on Three.js-related projects. Contributors can report issues, suggest enhancements, and submit pull requests to the official Three.js repository. This collaborative environment fosters innovation and ensures the continued improvement of the library.

- [Three.js Official Repository]*(https://github.com/mrdoob/three.js)*

- [Community-Contributed Three.js Extensions]*(https://github.com/community/three-extensions)*

- [Collaborative Three.js Art Projects]*(https://github.com/three-art/collaborations)*

Artistic Collaborations

Artists and developers often collaborate on projects that blend art and technology. Artists provide creative direction, while developers implement the technical aspects using Three.js. These collaborations result in groundbreaking digital art experiences that challenge conventions and inspire new forms of artistic expression.

// Example of an artist-developer collaboration in Three.js

```
const artist = {

vision: 'Create an immersive digital art piece',

style: 'Abstract and interactive',

};

const developer = {

expertise: 'Three.js, WebVR, JavaScript',

implementation: 'Bring the artist's vision to life using Three.js',

};
```

Creative Coding Communities

Online communities and forums dedicated to creative coding and Three.js offer spaces for members to share their work, seek feedback, and collaborate on projects. These communities provide inspiration, support, and a sense of belonging for individuals passionate about blending code and art.

- [Creative Coding Subreddit](*https://www.reddit.com/r/creativecoding/*)

- [Three.js Community Forum](*https://discourse.threejs.org/*)

- [WebGL Artisans Collective](*https://webglart.org/*)

Hackathons and Events

Hackathons and events focused on Three.js and creative coding gather like-minded individuals for intense periods of collaboration and creation. Participants often develop innovative projects, experiment with new techniques, and push the boundaries of what is possible with Three.js.

- [Three.js Creative Coding Hackathon]*(https://example.com/threejs-hackathon)*

- [WebGL Art Jam]*(https://example.com/webgl-art-jam)*

- [Creative Coding Festival]*(https://example.com/creative-coding-fest)*

The Three.js community's collaborative spirit and commitment to open-source principles have transformed the library into a thriving ecosystem. Whether you're a developer seeking to contribute code, an artist exploring creative possibilities, or someone looking to learn and share knowledge, the Three.js community offers a welcoming and supportive environment. Together, community members continue to push the boundaries of 3D web graphics, opening up new avenues for creativity and expression.

Chapter 19: Future Trends and Developments

19.1 The Evolution of Web Graphics APIs

As we look toward the future of web graphics and Three.js, it's essential to consider the evolving landscape of web graphics APIs. These APIs underpin the technologies that enable 3D web graphics, and they continue to advance, shaping the way we interact with and experience 3D content on the web.

WebGL and WebGPU

WebGL, which powers Three.js, has been a foundational technology for 3D web graphics. However, its successor, WebGPU, is on the horizon. WebGPU is designed to provide even lower-level access to graphics hardware, enabling more efficient and powerful rendering. This evolution promises better performance and improved capabilities for 3D web applications.

```
// Example of using WebGPU with Three.js (future implementation)

const renderer = new THREE.WebGPURenderer();
```

WebXR and Immersive Experiences

WebXR (Web Extended Reality) is another significant trend in web graphics. It encompasses both virtual reality (VR) and augmented reality (AR) and aims to make immersive experiences more accessible on the web. Three.js has been at the forefront of WebXR development, enabling developers to create VR and AR content that can be experienced directly in web browsers.

```
// Example of creating a WebXR scene with Three.js
```

```
const xrScene = new THREE.XRScene();
```

Integration with Web3 and Blockchain

Web3 technologies and blockchain are becoming increasingly intertwined with web graphics. Three.js is poised to play a role in creating decentralized and immersive experiences within the emerging web3 ecosystem. This integration can enable new forms of ownership, digital assets, and interactions in virtual spaces.

```
// Example of a decentralized 3D asset marketplace using Three.js

const marketplace = new THREE.Web3Marketplace();
```

Sustainability and Optimization

Sustainability is a growing concern in web development, including web graphics. Future developments in Three.js will likely include optimizations for resource usage, reducing the environmental impact of 3D web applications. This may involve more efficient rendering techniques, better memory management, and optimizations for low-power devices.

```
// Example of a Three.js application optimized for low-power devices

const lowPowerApp = new THREE.LowPowerApp();
```

Expanding the Creative Palette

Future trends in web graphics will likely expand the creative palette for artists and developers. This may involve the integration of new technologies, such as AI-driven content generation, volumetric rendering, and advanced physics simulations. Three.js will continue to adapt to incorporate these innovations.

```
// Example of AI-generated 3D content in Three.js
```

```
const aiGeneratedScene = new THREE.AIGeneratedScene();
```

Collaborative and Networked Experiences

Collaborative and networked experiences are expected to become more prevalent in 3D web graphics. Developers will have the tools to create shared virtual spaces where users can interact and collaborate in real-time. Three.js will evolve to support these networked experiences seamlessly.

```
// Example of a collaborative 3D virtual workspace with Three.js

const collaborativeWorkspace = new
THREE.CollaborativeWorkspace();
```

The future of web graphics and Three.js holds exciting possibilities. As technologies like WebGPU, WebXR, web3, and sustainability considerations continue to shape the landscape, Three.js will adapt and remain a vital tool for creating immersive and interactive 3D web content. Whether you're a developer, artist, or enthusiast, staying informed about these trends will be crucial to harnessing the full potential of 3D web graphics in the years to come.

19.2 Emerging Technologies in 3D Web

The world of 3D web graphics is continuously evolving, driven by emerging technologies that promise to reshape the way we interact with digital content. In this section, we explore some of these technologies and their potential impact on the future of 3D web graphics.

WebAssembly (Wasm)

WebAssembly is a binary instruction format designed for high-performance execution on web browsers. It enables developers to run code written in languages like C, C++, and Rust at near-native speeds in web applications. While not exclusive to 3D graphics, WebAssembly has the potential to enhance the performance of Three.js and other 3D libraries, allowing for more complex and computationally intensive web-based 3D applications.

```
// Example of using WebAssembly with Three.js (potential future implementation)

const renderer = new THREE.WebAssemblyRenderer();
```

Real-Time Ray Tracing

Real-time ray tracing is a rendering technique that simulates the behavior of light rays as they interact with virtual objects in a scene. While traditionally associated with offline rendering due to its computational demands, advancements in hardware acceleration are making real-time ray tracing feasible on the web. This technology can bring photorealism and improved lighting effects to web-based 3D graphics.

```
// Example of real-time ray tracing in Three.js (potential future implementation)

const renderer = new THREE.RayTracingRenderer();
```

5G Connectivity

The rollout of 5G networks promises to revolutionize the web experience, including 3D web graphics. With faster and more reliable connections, 3D content can be streamed and loaded seamlessly, reducing latency and enabling high-quality, real-time interactions. This can enhance multiplayer gaming experiences, AR applications, and other 3D web content.

// Example of a 3D multiplayer game utilizing 5G connectivity with Three.js

const multiplayerGame = **new** THREE.MultiplayerGame({ network: '5G' });

AI-Driven Content Generation

Artificial intelligence (AI) and machine learning are increasingly being used to generate 3D content automatically. This includes the creation of 3D models, textures, animations, and even entire environments. Integrating AI-driven content generation into Three.js can empower developers and artists to create 3D web graphics more efficiently and creatively.

// Example of AI-generated 3D content in Three.js (potential future implementation)

const aiGeneratedScene = **new** THREE.AIGeneratedScene();

Spatial Audio

Spatial audio technology allows for more immersive soundscapes in 3D web graphics. It enables audio sources to have positional data, providing a sense of direction and distance to the listener. As web browsers continue to support spatial audio, Three.js can take advantage of this technology to enhance the realism of 3D web applications.

// Example of spatial audio integration in Three.js (potential future implementation)

const audioScene = **new** THREE.SpatialAudioScene();

Decentralized and Blockchain Integration

Blockchain technology is expanding its presence in the digital world, and this includes 3D web graphics. Decentralized applications (DApps) and Non-Fungible Tokens (NFTs) are increasingly used to represent ownership of digital assets, including 3D models and virtual spaces. Three.js may play a role in creating decentralized and blockchain-integrated 3D web applications.

```
// Example of a decentralized 3D asset marketplace using Three.js (potential future implementation)

const marketplace = new THREE.BlockchainMarketplace();
```

Accessibility Innovations

Web accessibility is a critical consideration in the development of 3D web graphics. Emerging technologies will likely bring innovations in making 3D content more accessible to individuals with disabilities. This can include features such as voice commands, haptic feedback, and improved screen reader support in Three.js-based applications.

```
// Example of accessibility features in a Three.js application (potential future implementation)

const accessibleApp = new THREE.AccessibleApp();
```

These emerging technologies are poised to shape the future of 3D web graphics, offering new possibilities for developers, artists, and users alike. As these technologies mature and become more accessible, Three.js will continue to evolve to harness their capabilities, opening up exciting avenues for creativity and innovation in the world of web-based 3D content.

19.3 Three.js in the Context of Web3 and Blockchain

Web3, often referred to as the third generation of the internet, is a paradigm shift that introduces decentralization and blockchain technology to web applications. In this section, we'll explore the role of Three.js in the context of Web3 and blockchain and how it contributes to the creation of decentralized and immersive web experiences.

Decentralized Applications (DApps)

Decentralized applications, or DApps, are a cornerstone of Web3. These applications leverage blockchain technology to operate without a central authority, providing transparency, security, and trustlessness. Three.js can be integrated into DApps to create immersive 3D interfaces and experiences that interact with smart contracts on the blockchain.

```
// Example of a Three.js-powered Web3 DApp
const dapp = new THREE.Web3DApp({
contract: '0x123abc...', // Smart contract address
userWallet: '0xuserwallet...', // User's wallet address
});
```

Non-Fungible Tokens (NFTs)

Non-Fungible Tokens (NFTs) are unique digital assets that are indivisible and represent ownership of a specific item, artwork, or collectible. Three.js can be used to showcase and visualize NFTs in

3D, allowing users to explore and interact with their digital assets in a virtual environment.

```
// Example of an NFT gallery with Three.js integration
const nftGallery = new THREE.NFTGallery({
userWallet: '0xuserwallet...', // User's wallet address
nftCollection: '0xnfthash...', // NFT collection contract address
});
```

Virtual Real Estate and Environments

Blockchain-based virtual worlds and metaverses are gaining traction in the Web3 ecosystem. Three.js can play a significant role in creating these virtual environments, where users can buy, build, and interact with digital assets, including virtual real estate and 3D objects.

```
// Example of a blockchain-based virtual world powered by Three.js
const virtualWorld = new THREE.BlockchainWorld({
userWallet: '0xuserwallet...', // User's wallet address
realEstateContract: '0xrealestate...', // Virtual real estate contract address
});
```

Ownership and Interoperability

Three.js can be used to ensure ownership and interoperability of 3D assets in the context of blockchain. Smart contracts can be implemented to verify ownership and enable secure transfers of 3D models and scenes. This ensures that users have control over their digital assets and can use them in various Web3 applications.

```
// Example of a Three.js asset ownership smart contract
const assetContract = new THREE.AssetContract({
asset: '0xassethash...', // 3D asset hash
owner: '0xownerwallet...', // Current owner's wallet address
});
```

Decentralized Identity and Authentication

Web3 introduces decentralized identity solutions, where users have control over their identity and personal data. Three.js can be used to create 3D avatars and representations of users within decentralized applications, ensuring that users' identities remain under their control.

```
// Example of a Three.js avatar within a decentralized identity system
const decentralizedAvatar = new THREE.DecentralizedAvatar({
userWallet: '0xuserwallet...', // User's wallet address
decentralizedIdentity: '0xidentityhash...', // Decentralized identity contract
});
```

Tokenized Gaming and Virtual Goods

Tokenization of in-game assets and virtual goods is a growing trend in the gaming industry within the Web3 context. Three.js can be used to render and visualize tokenized game assets, enabling players to trade, sell, and use these assets across different games and platforms.

```
// Example of a tokenized game with Three.js-rendered assets
const tokenizedGame = new THREE.TokenizedGame({
userWallet: '0xuserwallet...', // User's wallet address
gameAssets: '0xgameassets...', // Tokenized game assets contract
});
```

Transparency and Provenance

Blockchain technology provides transparency and provenance for digital assets. Three.js can display blockchain data to users, showing the history and ownership of 3D assets. This transparency builds trust and ensures the authenticity of digital content.

```
// Example of displaying asset provenance with Three.js
const assetProvenance = new THREE.AssetProvenance({
asset: '0xassethash...', // 3D asset hash
blockchainData: '0xblockchaindata...', // Provenance data from blockchain
});
```

Three.js, with its capabilities in 3D graphics and web development, aligns well with the principles of decentralization, ownership, and immersion in the Web3 era. It offers the tools and flexibility needed to create engaging and interactive 3D web experiences that leverage the potential of blockchain technology and decentralized applications. As Web3 continues to evolve, Three.js is likely to play a crucial role in shaping the future of decentralized and immersive web applications.

19.4 Sustainable Development in 3D Web

Sustainability is an increasingly important consideration in all aspects of technology development, including 3D web graphics. As the demand for immersive and interactive 3D experiences grows, so does the need to minimize the environmental impact of such applications. In this section, we'll explore the concept of sustainable development in the context of 3D web graphics and how Three.js can contribute to more environmentally friendly practices.

Efficient Rendering Techniques

One way to achieve sustainability in 3D web development is by employing efficient rendering techniques. Three.js can optimize the rendering pipeline to reduce resource consumption, including CPU and GPU usage. This optimization minimizes the energy required to render 3D scenes, making applications more sustainable.

```
// Example of using efficient rendering techniques in Three.js

const renderer = new THREE.OptimizedRenderer();
```

Asset Optimization

Optimizing 3D assets such as models, textures, and animations is crucial for sustainable development. Three.js can integrate asset compression and simplification techniques to reduce the file size of 3D assets. Smaller asset sizes lead to faster loading times and less data transfer, resulting in lower energy consumption.

```
// Example of asset optimization in Three.js
```

```
const optimizedModel = new THREE.OptimizedModel({
sourceModel: '3dmodel.obj',
});
```

Performance Monitoring and Profiling

Sustainable development also involves monitoring and optimizing performance. Three.js can incorporate tools for real-time performance monitoring, allowing developers to identify resource-intensive areas and make improvements. This proactive approach helps ensure that applications remain energy-efficient.

```
// Example of performance monitoring in Three.js
const performanceMonitor = new THREE.PerformanceMonitor();
```

Dark Mode and Energy Efficiency

Implementing dark mode or energy-efficient rendering modes can further contribute to sustainability in 3D web graphics. Three.js can include features that adapt the rendering style to reduce the energy consumption of the device, especially for OLED screens, which are prevalent in modern devices.

```
// Example of dark mode rendering in Three.js
const darkModeRenderer = new THREE.DarkModeRenderer();
```

Low-Power Device Optimization

Optimizing 3D web applications for low-power devices, such as smartphones and tablets, is essential for sustainability. Three.js can provide tools and guidelines for developers to ensure that their applications run efficiently on these devices, extending battery life and reducing energy consumption.

```
// Example of a low-power device-optimized Three.js application

const lowPowerApp = new THREE.LowPowerApp();
```

Renewable Energy Hosting

Sustainable development extends beyond code and graphics to hosting infrastructure. Developers can choose hosting providers that use renewable energy sources, further reducing the environmental impact of web applications built with Three.js.

```
// Example of hosting on a renewable energy-powered server

const hostedApp = new THREE.HostedApp({

hostingProvider: 'renewable-energy-hosting.com',

});
```

Education and Awareness

Three.js can also play a role in raising awareness about sustainability in 3D web development. Tutorials and documentation can include best practices for sustainable design, helping developers make informed choices that reduce the ecological footprint of their applications.

- [Sustainable 3D Web Development Guide](https://example.com/sustainable-web-dev)

- [Eco-Friendly 3D Graphics with Three.js](https://example.com/eco-friendly-3d-graphics)

Collaborative Efforts

Sustainability is a collective effort, and the Three.js community can collaborate to develop and promote sustainable practices. Sharing knowledge, tools, and success stories related to sustainable 3D web development can inspire others to follow suit.

- [Sustainable Web Graphics Forum](*https://example.com/sustainable-graphics-forum*)

- [Community Challenges for Sustainable 3D Web](*https://example.com/sustainable-web-challenges*)

As sustainability becomes a more prominent concern in technology and web development, Three.js has the potential to lead the way in creating environmentally friendly 3D web experiences. By incorporating energy-efficient techniques, optimizing assets, and fostering a culture of sustainability, Three.js can contribute to a more sustainable future for 3D web graphics.

19.5 Predictions for the Future of Three.js

The future of Three.js holds exciting possibilities as it continues to evolve in response to emerging technologies, user demands, and industry trends. In this section, we'll explore some predictions for the future of Three.js and how it may shape the world of 3D web graphics.

1. Enhanced Performance

As hardware and web technologies advance, Three.js is likely to continue optimizing its rendering pipeline for better performance. This includes leveraging new browser features and hardware capabilities to deliver smoother and more responsive 3D experiences.

```
// Example of future performance optimizations in Three.js

const renderer = new THREE.AdvancedRenderer();
```

2. WebGPU Integration

With the adoption of WebGPU, Three.js may introduce native WebGPU support, taking advantage of lower-level access to the GPU for even faster rendering and more realistic graphics.

```
// Example of native WebGPU integration in a future version of Three.js

const renderer = new THREE.WebGPURenderer();
```

3. Real-Time Ray Tracing

The integration of real-time ray tracing techniques into Three.js could bring photorealism and enhanced lighting effects to web-based 3D graphics, further blurring the line between offline and real-time rendering.

```
// Example of real-time ray tracing in future versions of Three.js

const renderer = new THREE.RayTracingRenderer();
```

4. AI-Powered Tools

As AI and machine learning technologies advance, Three.js may incorporate AI-powered tools for content creation, including automatic generation of 3D models, textures, animations, and even entire scenes.

```
// Example of AI-generated content tools in future Three.js versions

const aiContentTools = new THREE.AIPoweredTools();
```

5. VR and AR Integration

With the growing interest in virtual reality (VR) and augmented reality (AR), Three.js is likely to continue leading the way in making immersive web experiences accessible and user-friendly.

```
// Example of future VR and AR integration in Three.js

const vrScene = new THREE.VRScene();
```

6. Blockchain and Web3 Integration

As blockchain technology becomes more ingrained in web development, Three.js may provide out-of-the-box solutions for integrating decentralized applications (DApps), non-fungible tokens (NFTs), and blockchain interactions into 3D web experiences.

```
// Example of Three.js with built-in blockchain integration in the future

const blockchainApp = new THREE.BlockchainApp();
```

7. Collaborative and Networked Environments

Three.js is likely to continue enabling the creation of collaborative and networked 3D environments, where users can interact, collaborate, and socialize in real-time, making web-based 3D experiences even more engaging.

```
// Example of collaborative and networked 3D environments in future Three.js

const collaborativeWorld = new THREE.CollaborativeWorld();
```

8. Accessibility Focus

As inclusivity and accessibility become central concerns, Three.js may introduce features and guidelines to make 3D web graphics more accessible to users with disabilities, including voice commands, haptic feedback, and improved screen reader support.

```
// Example of accessibility features in future Three.js versions

const accessibleApp = new THREE.AccessibleApp();
```

9. Environmental Sustainability

Sustainability is expected to be a significant theme in the future of Three.js. The framework may place a stronger emphasis on sustainable development practices, including energy-efficient rendering, asset optimization, and renewable hosting.

```
// Example of sustainability-focused features in future Three.js

const sustainableApp = new THREE.SustainableApp();
```

10. Continued Community Growth

The Three.js community is likely to continue growing, with developers, artists, and enthusiasts contributing to its success. This collaborative spirit will result in an ever-expanding library of resources, tutorials, and extensions.

- [Three.js Community Hub]*(https://example.com/threejs-community)*

- [Three.js Future Development Forum]*(https://example.com/threejs-future)*

These predictions offer a glimpse into the exciting future of Three.js and its role in shaping the world of 3D web graphics. As technology evolves and user expectations change, Three.js is poised to remain a powerful and innovative tool for creating immersive and interactive web experiences. Developers and creators can look forward to a future where Three.js continues to push the boundaries of what's possible in 3D web development.

20. Building a Complete Three.js Project

20.1 Planning and Structuring Your Project

Building a complete Three.js project involves not only mastering the technical aspects of Three.js but also carefully planning and structuring your project to ensure its success. In this section, we'll explore the essential steps and considerations for planning and structuring a Three.js project.

Define Your Project Goals

Before diving into code, it's crucial to define the goals and objectives of your Three.js project. What kind of 3D experience are you trying to create? Who is your target audience? What problem or need does your project address? Having a clear vision will guide your decisions throughout the development process.

Choose the Right Three.js Version

Three.js is actively developed, and new versions are released regularly. Ensure you're using a version that suits your project's needs. Newer versions may introduce performance improvements, bug fixes, and new features, while older versions might be more stable for certain projects.

```
// Specify the Three.js version in your project's package.json

{

"dependencies": {

"three": "^0.135.0"
```

```
}
}
```

Project Structure

Organizing your project's structure is crucial for maintainability and collaboration. Consider using a folder structure that separates assets, scripts, styles, and configuration files. This separation makes it easier to find and manage your code and resources.

```
project/
├── assets/
│ ├── models/
│ ├── textures/
│ ├── audio/
├── scripts/
│ ├── main.js
│ ├── utils/
├── styles/
│ ├── main.css
├── index.html
```

Version Control

Use version control systems like Git to track changes in your project. Hosting your code on platforms like GitHub, GitLab, or Bitbucket allows for collaboration with others and provides a safety net in case of errors or data loss.

 # Initialize a Git repository for your project

git init

Project Dependencies

Depending on your project's requirements, you may need additional libraries or modules. Utilize package managers like npm or yarn to manage and install dependencies easily.

 # Install Three.js and other dependencies using npm

npm install three

Build and Bundling Tools

Consider using build tools like webpack or Parcel to bundle your JavaScript, CSS, and assets efficiently. These tools can optimize your code for production, handle minification, and reduce load times.

// Example webpack configuration for Three.js project

module.exports = {

entry: './src/main.js',

output: {

filename: 'bundle.js',

path: path.resolve(__dirname, 'dist'),

},

};

Continuous Integration (CI)

Implement continuous integration tools to automate testing and deployment processes. Services like Travis CI or GitHub Actions can help ensure the quality and stability of your project.

```
# Example GitHub Actions workflow for Three.js project

name: Build and Deploy

on:

push:

branches:

- main

jobs:

build:

runs-on: ubuntu-latest

steps:

- name: Checkout code

uses: actions/checkout@v2

- name: Install dependencies

run: npm install

- name: Build project

run: npm run build

- name: Deploy to hosting
```

run: |

Add deployment script here

Documentation

Maintain clear and comprehensive documentation for your project. Document code, APIs, and usage instructions to make it easier for collaborators and users to understand and contribute to your project.

- *[*Project Documentation*](https://example.com/project-docs)*

- *[*Three.js API Reference*](https://threejs.org/docs/index.html)*

Testing and Quality Assurance

Implement testing procedures to catch bugs and ensure the reliability of your project. Tools like Jest or Mocha can be used for unit testing, and frameworks like Puppeteer for end-to-end testing of 3D interactions.

```
// Example unit test using Jest

test('Model loading', () => {

const model = new THREE.ModelLoader();

expect(model.load('model.gltf')).toBeInstanceOf(THREE.Mesh);

});
```

Deployment

Choose a hosting environment that suits your project's needs. Whether it's a static file host, a cloud service, or a dedicated server, ensure your project is accessible to users.

```
# Deploy your project to a hosting platform

npm run deploy
```

By carefully planning and structuring your Three.js project, you set a strong foundation for successful development. Consider your project's goals, choose the right tools, organize your code, and prioritize documentation and testing. With these elements in place, you'll be well-prepared to create and maintain a complete Three.js project that meets your vision and the needs of your audience.

20.2 Developing a Comprehensive 3D Application

Developing a comprehensive 3D application with Three.js involves more than just rendering 3D models. It requires building interactive and engaging user experiences. In this section, we'll explore the key steps and considerations for creating a complete 3D application using Three.js.

User Interface Design

Start by designing the user interface (UI) for your 3D application. Consider how users will interact with the 3D scene, what controls and buttons are needed, and how information will be presented. You can use standard HTML elements alongside your Three.js canvas to create an intuitive UI.

```
<!—Example HTML structure for integrating UI with Three.js—>

<div id="app-container">

<canvas id="threejs-canvas"></canvas>

<div id="ui-container">
```

```
<button id="start-button">Start</button>

<div id="info-panel">

<p>Score: <span id="score">0</span></p>

</div>

</div>

</div>
```

User Interaction

Implement user interaction within your 3D scene. Three.js provides event listeners to capture mouse and touch events, allowing users to interact with objects in the 3D environment. You can define actions such as object selection, camera movement, and scene manipulation based on user input.

```
// Example of adding a click event listener in Three.js

const object = new THREE.Mesh(geometry, material);

object.addEventListener('click', () => {

// Perform actions when the object is clicked

console.log('Object clicked!');

});
```

Animation and Scene Logic

Bring your 3D scene to life with animations and scene logic. Use keyframe animations, physics simulations, or custom scripts to create dynamic and engaging experiences. Think about how objects should move, react to user input, and trigger events within the scene.

```
// Example of keyframe animation in Three.js

const animation = new THREE.AnimationMixer(object);

const clip = THREE.AnimationClip.findByName(animations, 'walk');

const action = animation.clipAction(clip);

action.play();
```

Data Management

If your 3D application involves data, consider how to manage and display it effectively. Whether it's loading external data sources, parsing JSON files, or connecting to APIs, handling data efficiently is crucial for a comprehensive application.

```
// Example of loading external JSON data in Three.js

fetch('data.json')

.then((response) => response.json())

.then((data) => {

// Process and use the data in your application

console.log(data);

});
```

Performance Optimization

Optimize your 3D application for performance. This includes optimizing rendering, reducing unnecessary calculations, and using techniques like level-of-detail (LOD) to manage complex scenes efficiently. High performance ensures a smooth user experience, even on less powerful devices.

```
// Example of implementing level-of-detail in Three.js

const lod = new THREE.LOD();

lod.addLevel(highDetailMesh, 0);

lod.addLevel(mediumDetailMesh, 500);

lod.addLevel(lowDetailMesh, 1000);

scene.add(lod);
```

Testing and Debugging

Thoroughly test and debug your 3D application to catch issues and ensure a stable user experience. Use browser developer tools, console logging, and debugging libraries to identify and resolve errors. Additionally, consider user testing to gather feedback and make improvements.

```
// Example of using console.log() for debugging in Three.js

console.log('Debug message:', variableToInspect);
```

Cross-Browser Compatibility

Ensure that your 3D application works smoothly across different web browsers and devices. Test your application on popular browsers like Chrome, Firefox, Safari, and Edge, and consider using tools like BrowserStack for cross-browser compatibility testing.

- [BrowserStack](https://www.browserstack.com/)

Deployment and Hosting

Choose an appropriate hosting solution to deploy your 3D application. Depending on your project, you may opt for static file hosting, cloud services, or dedicated servers. Ensure that your hosting environment can handle the traffic and resource requirements of your application.

 # Deploy your 3D application to a web hosting platform

npm run deploy

User Documentation

Provide user documentation and instructions on how to use your 3D application. Explain the controls, features, and any user-specific actions they need to take to fully experience your application.

- [Application User Guide](*https://example.com/user-guide*)

- [Frequently Asked Questions](*https://example.com/faq*)

Developing a comprehensive 3D application with Three.js is a rewarding but complex endeavor. By carefully planning your user interface, implementing user interaction, animations, and scene logic, managing data, optimizing performance, testing, ensuring cross-browser compatibility, and providing user documentation, you can create a rich and engaging 3D experience for your audience.

20.3 Testing and Debugging Strategies

Testing and debugging are essential aspects of developing a complete Three.js project. Ensuring that your 3D application functions as expected and identifying and resolving issues are critical for delivering a high-quality user experience. In this section, we'll explore various testing and debugging strategies you can employ in your Three.js project.

Console Logging

Console logging is a fundamental debugging technique. You can use console.log(), console.error(), and console.warn() to output messages and variables to the browser's developer console. This helps you inspect values, trace code execution, and identify errors.

// Example of using console.log() for debugging in Three.js

console.log('Debug message:', variableToInspect);

Browser Developer Tools

Modern web browsers provide developer tools that are powerful for debugging Three.js applications. You can inspect the Three.js scene graph, view rendering performance, and access the console for debugging messages. Familiarize yourself with the browser's developer tools for effective debugging.

Debugging Libraries

Consider using debugging libraries specifically designed for Three.js development. Libraries like THREE.DebugUtils provide additional debugging functionalities, such as visualizing bounding boxes and axes, which can help you understand the scene's structure.

// Example of using THREE.DebugUtils in Three.js

THREE.DebugUtils.makeDebug(scene);

Unit Testing

Unit testing allows you to test individual components or functions of your Three.js project in isolation. Frameworks like Jest or Mocha can be used for writing and running unit tests. You can test functions, utilities, and mathematical calculations to ensure correctness.

```
// Example unit test using Jest for a Three.js function

test('Object rotation', () => {

const object = new THREE.Mesh();

rotateObject(object, Math.PI / 2);

expect(object.rotation.x).toBeCloseTo(Math.PI / 2);

});
```

End-to-End Testing

End-to-end testing involves simulating user interactions and verifying that your application functions correctly as a whole. Tools like Puppeteer can be used to automate user actions and capture screenshots or analyze the rendered output.

```
// Example end-to-end test using Puppeteer for Three.js interaction

const puppeteer = require('puppeteer');

(async () => {

const browser = await puppeteer.launch();

const page = await browser.newPage();

await page.goto('https://example.com/your-3d-app');
```

```
// Simulate user interactions and perform assertions
await browser.close();
})();
```

Performance Profiling

Performance profiling tools like the Chrome DevTools Performance panel can help you identify bottlenecks and optimize your Three.js project for better rendering speed. Profile your application's performance to find areas where improvements are needed.

Error Handling

Implement proper error handling in your Three.js project. Use try-catch blocks to capture and handle exceptions gracefully. Display user-friendly error messages and log detailed information to the console to assist with debugging.

```
// Example of error handling in Three.js code
try {
// Code that may throw an error
} catch (error) {
console.error('An error occurred:', error);
// Display an error message to the user
}
```

Continuous Integration (CI)

Integrate continuous integration (CI) tools into your project's workflow. CI services like Travis CI or GitHub Actions can automatically run tests, build, and deploy your Three.js application when changes are pushed to your version control repository. This ensures that new code doesn't introduce regressions.

```
# Example GitHub Actions workflow for Three.js project

name: Build and Test

on:

push:

branches:

- main

jobs:

build:

runs-on: ubuntu-latest

steps:

- name: Checkout code

uses: actions/checkout@v2

- name: Install dependencies

run: npm install

- name: Run tests

run: npm test
```

User Testing

User testing is valuable for gathering feedback and identifying usability issues in your Three.js application. Involve potential users to interact with your application and provide insights into their experience. User testing can reveal issues that you might have overlooked.

Version Control and Debugging

Version control systems like Git play a significant role in debugging. You can use Git's version history to track down when an issue was introduced and which code changes may have caused it. By reviewing commit logs, you can pinpoint the source of problems and revert to a working state if necessary.

```
# Use Git to check commit history and identify issues

git log
```

Testing and debugging are ongoing processes throughout your Three.js project's development lifecycle. By employing a combination of techniques, including console logging, browser developer tools, debugging libraries, unit testing, end-to-end testing, performance profiling, error handling, continuous integration, user testing, and version control, you can ensure that your 3D application is robust, reliable, and user-friendly.

20.4 Deployment and Hosting Considerations

Deploying and hosting your Three.js project is a crucial step in making your 3D application accessible to users on the web. In this section, we'll explore important considerations and strategies for deploying and hosting your Three.js project effectively.

Choosing a Hosting Service

Selecting the right hosting service depends on your project's requirements and budget. Consider the following hosting options:

1. **Static File Hosting:** Services like Netlify, Vercel, and GitHub Pages are excellent choices for hosting static websites and Three.js applications. They offer simple deployment workflows and often provide free plans.
2. **Cloud Hosting:** Cloud providers like AWS, Azure, and Google Cloud offer scalable hosting solutions suitable for large-scale projects. You can set up virtual machines, containers, or serverless functions to serve your application.
3. **Dedicated Server:** If you have specific server requirements or need full control over your hosting environment, you can opt for dedicated server hosting from providers like DigitalOcean or Linode.
4. **Content Delivery Network (CDN):** CDNs like Cloudflare or Akamai can improve the global distribution and performance of your application by caching and serving assets from multiple data centers worldwide.

Domain Name

Register a domain name for your Three.js project to make it accessible through a memorable and branded URL. Many hosting services offer domain registration as part of their services. Ensure that your domain name reflects your project's identity.

SSL/TLS Security

Secure your Three.js application with SSL/TLS encryption to protect user data and build trust. Many hosting providers offer free SSL certificates through services like Let's Encrypt. Enabling HTTPS is essential, especially if your application handles sensitive information.

Deployment Workflow

Establish a deployment workflow that streamlines the process of pushing updates to your live application. Use version control and continuous integration (CI) tools to automate testing, building, and deployment. This ensures that changes are deployed consistently and reliably.

```
# Example GitHub Actions workflow for deploying a Three.js project

name: Build and Deploy

on:

push:

branches:

- main

jobs:

build:

runs-on: ubuntu-latest

steps:

- name: Checkout code
```

```
uses: actions/checkout@v2

- name: Install dependencies

run: npm install

- name: Build project

run: npm run build

- name: Deploy to hosting

run: |

# Add deployment script here
```

Asset Optimization

Optimize your Three.js project's assets, such as 3D models, textures, and images, to reduce loading times. Use tools like TinyPNG for image compression, and consider utilizing asset pipelines to preprocess and compress assets before deployment.

Cache Control

Implement cache control headers to control how assets are cached in the user's browser. Proper cache management can improve page load times for returning visitors. Consider using cache-busting techniques to ensure that updated assets are fetched when you make changes.

Content Delivery

Leverage content delivery networks (CDNs) to distribute your assets globally. CDNs can significantly improve loading times by serving content from geographically distributed servers. Ensure that your CDN is configured to cache and deliver Three.js assets efficiently.

Monitoring and Analytics

Implement monitoring and analytics tools to gain insights into your application's performance and user behavior. Services like Google Analytics or New Relic can help you track user interactions, identify bottlenecks, and make data-driven optimizations.

Backup and Redundancy

Regularly back up your Three.js project and its data to prevent data loss. Consider implementing redundancy measures to ensure high availability in case of server failures. Automated backup solutions and failover mechanisms can be invaluable.

Scalability

Plan for scalability by choosing a hosting solution that can handle increased traffic as your application grows. Cloud providers offer autoscaling features that automatically adjust resources based on demand, helping you maintain performance during traffic spikes.

Cost Management

Keep an eye on hosting costs and optimize resources to stay within budget. Monitor resource usage, and consider reserved instances or cost-effective server configurations to reduce expenses while maintaining performance.

Deploying and hosting your Three.js project requires careful planning and consideration of factors such as hosting options, domain names, security, deployment workflows, asset optimization, cache control, content delivery, monitoring, backups, scalability, and cost management. By addressing these considerations, you can ensure that your 3D application is accessible, secure, and performant for your users.

20.5 Post-Launch Maintenance and Updates

Launching your Three.js project is a significant achievement, but the work doesn't end there. Post-launch maintenance and updates are essential to ensure that your 3D application remains functional, secure, and relevant. In this section, we'll explore key considerations for maintaining and updating your Three.js project.

Bug Fixes

Even with thorough testing, it's common for bugs to surface after the initial launch. Monitor user feedback and error reports to identify and fix issues promptly. Maintain a bug tracking system to prioritize and address reported problems efficiently.

- [Bug Tracking System](https://example.com/bug-tracker)

Security Updates

Stay vigilant about security vulnerabilities. Regularly update dependencies, including Three.js and any third-party libraries, to patch known security issues. Implement security best practices and follow security guidelines to protect user data and the integrity of your application.

Browser Compatibility

Web browsers evolve over time, and new versions may introduce changes that affect the compatibility of your Three.js project. Periodically test your application on different browsers and update code or dependencies to ensure consistent performance and functionality.

Performance Optimization

Continuously optimize the performance of your Three.js application. Profile and analyze performance metrics to identify bottlenecks and areas for improvement. Implement performance enhancements, such as optimizing asset loading and reducing rendering overhead.

Content Updates

Keep your content fresh and engaging to retain user interest. Regularly update 3D models, textures, and any interactive elements to provide new experiences. Announce updates or new features to your user base to encourage engagement.

Compatibility with New Three.js Versions

Three.js releases updates with new features and improvements. Stay informed about new releases and their potential impact on your project. Plan for compatibility updates and take advantage of new Three.js features to enhance your application.

// Example of updating to a new Three.js version

npm install three@latest

Backup and Disaster Recovery

Maintain robust backup and disaster recovery procedures. Regularly back up your application and data to secure locations. Establish recovery plans to minimize downtime in case of unexpected incidents, such as server failures or data breaches.

User Support and Documentation

Provide ongoing user support through channels like email, chat, or forums. Maintain user documentation and FAQs to assist users with common questions and issues. A well-supported application fosters user satisfaction and loyalty.

- [User Support](*https://example.com/support*)

- [Frequently Asked Questions](*https://example.com/faq*)

Analytics and User Feedback

Continue monitoring user behavior and feedback after the launch. Analytics tools can help you gain insights into user interactions and preferences. Use this data to make informed decisions about updates and improvements.

Version Control and Testing

Maintain a version control system to track changes and collaborate with team members effectively. Implement testing practices, including regression testing, to ensure that updates and new features do not introduce regressions or break existing functionality.

Compliance and Regulations

Stay informed about legal and regulatory changes that may affect your application. Ensure that your Three.js project complies with data protection, accessibility, and other relevant laws and regulations. Make necessary adjustments to remain in compliance.

User Engagement and Marketing

Promote your Three.js project to attract new users and retain existing ones. Engage with your user community through social media, newsletters, and announcements. Consider running marketing campaigns or collaborations to increase visibility.

- [Follow us on Twitter](*https://twitter.com/your-3d-app*)

- [Subscribe to our Newsletter](*https://example.com/newsletter*)

Post-launch maintenance and updates are essential for the long-term success of your Three.js project. By addressing bug fixes, security updates, browser compatibility, performance optimization, content updates, Three.js version compatibility, backup and recovery, user support, documentation, analytics, version control, compliance, user engagement, and marketing, you can ensure that your 3D application continues to deliver value and a positive user experience.

www.ingramcontent.com/pod-product-compliance
Lightning Source LLC
LaVergne TN
LVHW090258210926
848480LV00001B/67
* 9 7 9 8 2 2 3 8 5 4 8 1 4 *